C0-CCN-117

FOR THE CIVIC GOOD

THE NEW PUBLIC SCHOLARSHIP

SERIES EDITORS

Lonnie Bunch, *Director, National Museum of African-American History and Culture*
Julie Ellison, *Professor of American Culture, University of Michigan*
Robert Weisbuch, *President, Drew University*

The New Public Scholarship encourages alliances between scholars and communities by publishing writing that emerges from publicly engaged and intellectually consequential cultural work. The series is designed to attract serious readers who are invested in both creating and thinking about public culture and public life. Under the rubric of "public scholar," we embrace campus-based artists, humanists, cultural critics, and engaged artists working in the public, nonprofit, or private sector. The editors seek useful work growing out of engaged practices in cultural and educational arenas. We are also interested in books that offer new paradigms for doing and theorizing public scholarship itself. Indeed, validating public scholarship through an evolving set of concepts and arguments is central to **The New Public Scholarship.**

The universe of potential contributors and readers is growing rapidly. We are teaching a generation of students for whom civic education and community service learning are quite normative. The civic turn in art and design has affected educational and cultural institutions of many kinds. In light of these developments, we feel that **The New Public Scholarship** offers a timely innovation in serious publishing.

Civic Engagement in the Wake of Katrina, edited by Amy Koritz and
George J. Sanchez

Is William Martinez Not Our Brother?: Twenty Years of the Prison Creative Arts Project, Buzz Alexander

The Word on the Street: Linking the Academy and the Common Reader, Harvey Teres

For the Civic Good: The Liberal Case for Teaching Religion in the Public Schools,
Walter Feinberg and Richard A. Layton

For the Civic Good

THE LIBERAL CASE FOR TEACHING RELIGION IN THE PUBLIC SCHOOLS

Walter Feinberg and
Richard A. Layton

TOURO COLLEGE LIBRARY
Kings Hwy

The University of Michigan Press
Ann Arbor

KH

Copyright © by the University of Michigan 2014
All rights reserved

This book may not be reproduced, in whole or in part, including illustrations, in any form (beyond that copying permitted by Sections 107 and 108 of the U.S. Copyright Law and except by reviewers for the public press), without written permission from the publisher.

Published in the United States of America by
The University of Michigan Press
Manufactured in the United States of America
⊚ Printed on acid-free paper

2017   2016   2015   2014   4   3   2   1

A CIP catalog record for this book is available from the British Library.

ISBN 978-0-472-07207-1 (cloth : alk. paper)
ISBN 978-0-472-05207-3 (paper : alk. paper)
ISBN 978-0-472-12000-0 (e-book)

9/8/15

ACKNOWLEDGMENTS

This book has been several years in the making, and we could not have accomplished it without the generous participation and support of a number of people. First and foremost, we would like to thank all the teachers and administrators who generously responded to our initial survey, who opened their classrooms to us, and spent many of their precious hours in interviews with us. The faculty and staff of the participating schools were always hospitable to us, despite the intrusions we made into the regular work of their school days.

We also thank Andrew Race, Seamus Mulryan, and Jeff Thibert, three graduate students who assisted in the early part of the project, helping us to contact schools, facilitate meetings, and transcribe sessions of our interviews and class observations. We owe a special debt of gratitude to Sara Shrader, another graduate student whose assistance was invaluable throughout the project. Sara traveled with us to observe classroom sessions, interviewed teachers along with us, and reviewed and edited earlier versions of the study. Her contribution to the study is reflected on every page of the book. All four students served, perhaps more frequently than they might have wished, as valuable sounding boards to test and refine our perceptions, judgments, and conclusions.

This study also depended on generous financial support. The initial survey of curricula for courses in religion in public schools was made possible by the support of the University of Illinois Research Board. The extensive field visits and interviews with participating school staff members were supported by a grant from the Spencer Foundation. The Department of Religion and the College of Education at the University of Illinois also enabled our research through the granting of leave time and the provision of grant support.

Finally, we would like to thank the two anonymous readers for their valuable observations and critique of an earlier draft, and Thomas Dwyer, Andrea Olson, and the dedicated staff of the University of Michigan Press for shepherding the book to its completion.

CONTENTS

Chapter 1

INTRODUCTION
The Liberal Case for Teaching Religion in Public Schools

The introduction of courses about religion can arouse strong passions with the potential to tear communities apart. In Odessa, Texas, for example, the community divided sharply over two potential Bible curricula proposed for the local high schools. The majority of the school board and constituents favored the curriculum *The Bible in History and Literature*, produced by the National Council on Bible Curriculum in Public Schools (NCBCPS), a yearlong plan for Bible study closely tied to evangelical Christian organizations. Opposition to this curriculum developed among a small group of parents and teachers, including several members of the textbook-selection committee appointed by the school board. These opponents suggested instead that the board adopt the rival curriculum and textbook of the Bible Literacy Project (BLP). As the school board met to make the final decision on the district's curriculum, pressure mounted both inside and outside the meeting hall. One board member stated that he had received 140 phone calls in the preceding weeks urging him to support the NCBCPS curriculum. Outside, the pressure was no less intense. Demonstrators milled in the streets and celebrated the adoption of *The Bible in History* with the civil rights–era hymn, "Victory is mine, Victory is mine, Victory today is mine," they sang, "I told Satan, Get thee behind, Victory today is mine."[1] That victory, however, was short lived. Parents filed a suit against the school district on grounds that the adoption of the course violated the establishment clause of the First Amendment. As part of the ultimate settlement of the suit, the district agreed to remove the contested curriculum in favor of a modified course adopting neither of the two rival curricula.

At about the same time as the dramatic Odessa school board vote, a comparable spectacle was unfolding in the chambers of the Alabama state legislature. The Democratic majority had submitted a bill establishing a Bible elective stipulating the BLP's *The Bible and Its Influence* as the approved textbook. If passed and signed by the governor, such a bill would deprive the NCBCPS of an opportunity for placement in Alabama schools. Republicans, powerless to pass their own bill, turned to obstruction. As Amy Sullivan vividly reports, in February 2006, Republican legislators "took to the crimson-carpeted floor of the state house" to do "everything in their procedural power to stop" the establishment of the BLP-based elective, "even if that meant lining up to explain why they could not—could not!—stand for this attempt to bring a class about the Bible to the public schools."[2]

In these two cases, citizens, local administrators, and legislators found themselves pitted against each other on how to advance a goal all purportedly shared: to improve the biblical literacy of students in their communities. Odessa, Texas, and Montgomery, Alabama, are not isolated cases. In school-board meeting rooms, courthouses, and state capitols around the country, communities repeat acrimonious encounters. In these conflicted environments, the distinctive mission of the public school, which has commitments to students from different religious backgrounds (or from none at all), is muted by the cacophony of political voices.

Yet these are voices of distraction and the stridency of these disputes points to the need for a clear discussion of the potential *educational* value of such courses, and clearly education is not served by making the schools an adjunct to any church or set of beliefs or nonbeliefs. Without a robust discussion about the distinctive role of education, decisions will continue to be directed by the exercise of political power rather than by the educational needs of the students, the demands of the subject matter, and the informed consideration of educators. Nevertheless, given these conflicts it is not surprising that many educators are gun-shy about teaching anything that smacks of religion. Still, America's recent religious revival permeates all aspects of public life and has been especially prominent in debates about education.

Two issues—the teaching of creationism or intelligent design as an alternative to evolution and the constitutionality of providing public support to children for attending religious schools—have received the most attention. Less visible has been a persistent movement, fostered by well-financed national interest groups, to promote the teaching of Bible and religion courses in the public schools. We recognize that the terms "religion course" and "teach religion" are problematic and will clarify what we mean by them in the pages that follow. For some, the idea of teaching religion in the public schools is un-American, violating in spirit, if not in letter, the First Amendment. For others it is an affirmation of America's religious roots and a way to navigate around court rulings against the devotional teaching of religion. For others still, it is a critical academic subject that can guide students through confusing terrain in troubled times.

The controversy suggests that a more robust discussion of educational aims is needed, and, in and of itself, controversy is not a sufficient reason for rejecting an important subject. Ever since the Civil War, the question of the place of religion in schools has been associated with conflicting visions of America. To allow the specters of these conflicts to haunt the present discussion suggests a lack of imagination where both sides assume, one in positive tones, the other in negative, that instruction about religion must inevitably involve indoctrination and that hence it is a subject to be avoided by schools. The resolution requires an understanding of the unique role that public education should be expected to play in a liberal, democratic society.

TWO LIBERAL ARGUMENTS

From the point of view of liberal theory, there are two powerful justifications for introducing religion courses into public schools. The first is that courses about religion are important for the development of student autonomy; the second is that such courses are important to improve the quality of civic participation. There are other reasons for teaching religion that we explore in this book, but these are often extraneous to the aims of education in a liberal democracy.

The first justification follows from a certain understanding of autonomy as the capacity to choose and to revise one's conception of the good, that is, that autonomy does not develop spontaneously, but that children must be educated into autonomy. This requires three things: first, an understanding of the traditions out of which prevalent conceptions of the good arise; second, the willingness to own one of these conceptions in light of others; third, a developed capacity to recognize and reflect upon one's inherited conception of the good. Educational theorists have traditionally held that a good education must avoid manipulating students' beliefs, and, insofar as possible, must avoid indoctrinating them. But this is only a negative injunction, telling schools what they must not do, assuming that autonomy will develop by itself. Schools that aim to *promote* autonomy need to do more. They must provide the logical skills and the information necessary to assess different conceptions of the good.[3]

Religion *is* an important source of people's conception of the good, and to neglect to teach students about religion is to fail to provide them with the material they need for an intelligent revision of their own conception of the good. The failure of many public schools to offer courses in religion can be traced to two impulses. First, some conservatives hold that religious instruction should be the exclusive domain of the family, and second, many progressives fear that religion classes will be used to indoctrinate students. Certainly, as we document in this book, problems can arise when religion is taught in such a way as to make it difficult for students to evaluate the conceptions of the good that it offers—when in subtle or not so subtle ways they are indoctrinated and manipulated. However, as we also document, it need not be taught in this way.

The second liberal argument for teaching religion involves the requirements of a democratic public in the postmodern age. A democratic civic public arises when people from different traditions engage with one another in the construction of meaning and the building of a common future, and it is the unique role of a public school to create such a public. At a time when different religions are playing such an important role in civic life throughout the world, citizenship and informed public participation require a greater understanding of the role religion plays in people's lives. As part of its unique mission, public schools have a responsibility to provide this understanding.

Other arguments have been provided for teaching religion courses in the public schools. Some of these—such as the claim that America is founded on biblical values—are clearly inconsistent with any reasonable idea of education in a postmodern society where religious and ethnic diversity is a fact of life and where respect is a basic educational requirement. This argument is also questionable on historical grounds. Other arguments, such as the need to improve religious literacy, have greater currency. Clearly, one of the key tasks of education is to introduce students to important institutions and great traditions. This is a reasonable aim. Nevertheless, we show that without clear liberal principles to guide this effort, teaching for religious literacy is subject to abuses, both legal and educational.

Despite the many difficulties that religion courses present, we also hold out the prospect that they could serve important civic ends and contribute to the construction of a democratic civic public. In our mind, a public education at its best is a process where future citizens learn to recognize strangers as inheriting a shared fate and as co-agents in building a common future, that is, building a democratic public. Although often an arena for sectarian interests, religion courses, taught by well-trained teachers as a part of the public school humanities curriculum, could serve this civic role.

In this book, we ask two seemingly simple questions: First, what value do teachers believe these courses serve? Second, are there any educational values that these courses might serve that could not be serviced in other ways, say, by more traditional courses, or by instruction within religious communities themselves? To answer these questions fairly we need to extend the benefit of the doubt to those who teach these courses and to extract possibilities that they might not always realize are present. At the same time, if the educational potential of these courses is to be realized it is important not to hide the difficulties, missteps, and problems that we find in the different schools that we study.

The term "religion course" is our general label for four different kinds of courses: Bible History, the Bible and Its Influence, Bible as Literature, and World Religions. We examine these types of courses separately in chapters 2–7. When taught in a public school, each of these courses may elicit some degree of controversy. While our study is unlikely to put this controversy to rest, we hope that it may provide a clearer sense of the appropriate role of religion courses in public education. Given the importance of religion in both American culture and in global connections, given the many misconceptions perpetrated about certain faith traditions, and given the difficulty that many people have in rationally discussing differences of faith and commitment, we will conclude that while often deeply problematic, these courses have the potential to make a unique and positive contribution to the civic role of public education.

RELIGION AND THE ROLE OF THE HUMANITIES

The humanities, where we believe religion courses should firmly be situated, should awaken students to the significance of interpretive and analytic skills. In addition, religion courses have the potential to add a reflective element to these skills. Here students may awaken to the fact of their own interpretive framework and how this framework influences their own understanding of texts and practices. Because autonomy must both be respected as well as developed, we argue that the proper aim of this awakening for religion courses in public schools is not to change belief, nor to encourage students to believe that all religions are of equal worth (although some students may conclude that they are). Rather, the aim of the humanities from a civic standpoint is to promote civic skills by changing the *process of believing* and thus preparing the ground for engaging different points of view in civically constructive ways.[4]

This is precisely what the humanities do in good literature or history courses, in which students learn to distinguish a primary text from its subsequent reception and to entertain competing interpretations. From this process, they can learn to acknowledge the contested nature of many claims, to draw tentative hypotheses about meaning, to differentiate the various functions texts fill for different audiences, and then to engage the shifting horizons of the different audiences. The entire process requires that students develop the capacity to reflect on their own understanding as they learn to engage each other through texts in more complex and refined ways. While few religion courses now fully reach this stage, the subject itself has tremendous potential for contributing to a reflective civic and civil discourse, and thus it has great potential for enhancing autonomy by providing students with an understanding of different interpretive possibilities that exist both within and between different communities. In part, this book is intended to illustrate that potential without obscuring the difficulties in realizing it. The chapters are arranged in terms of a progression toward self-reflection and preparation for civic engagement. Hence, the later chapters describe courses that come closer to meeting the humanities ideal than the earlier ones. In the early chapters, the teachers see the autonomy of students and their parents as a constraint, a line they should not cross. Whether or not they are successful in restraining themselves from crossing this line is part of our discussion in these chapters. Nevertheless, while they do attempt to respect the students' autonomy, they do not seek to develop it or to provide a basis that students could use to reflect on their own inherited tradition. We speculate that this kind of teaching will lead either to dogmatically held beliefs where students have difficulty entertaining different beliefs or to instability where students who encounter differences flee from their own beliefs. The classes described in the later chapters of this book exhibit teachers who want both to respect the students' present state as an autonomous being and to provide opportunities for these students to enhance their autonomy by expanding their capacity for interpretive and reflective engagement, a capacity that is likely to contribute to an integrated character and more expansive agency.[5]

Our research took place over a two-year period. During this time, we traveled from the Bible Belt to the suburban parkway, observing classes and interviewing public school teachers involved in religion courses. We spent time in all four types of classes and report on their comparative problems and successes. In reporting on each, we deconstruct existing practices in order to highlight the possibility they offer for educating a democratic public. We conclude with a conditional endorsement of the potential some of these courses offer, arguing that when properly taught by well trained, committed teachers they can make a unique contribution to American education. Nevertheless, while we hold to the claim that religion courses can advance individual growth and civic engagement, our endorsement of actual religion courses is reserved and tentative. If our study has shown us anything, it is just how difficult it is to find competent teachers committed to developing autonomy with regard to inherited conceptions of the good and enhancing the civic discourse among religious strangers—and how easy it is to find teachers who unconsciously perpetuate their own religious commitments in their classrooms. It is not hard, then, to understand why some schools are reluctant to teach religion courses and why many that do teach them do not do so in a way that enhances the civic discourse.

Nevertheless, the failure to teach religion is not due to a lack of interest on the part of students. As Noddings has shown, there is certainly intense student concern about religious questions.[6] Nor is it likely that most high-school students are not mature enough or intellectual enough to engage religious issues. A number of the teachers we interviewed told us that many students who are slow in other areas shine in their religion courses. Nor is the topic of religion unimportant. Indeed, some scholars argue that to fail to teach religion actually distorts and minimizes its significance.[7] Nor is there a lack of ideas about how to teach religion in a professionally competent way.[8] Still, one of the most telling paradoxes of American education is the reluctance of many schools to teach the most canonical of all books in the Western traditions, the Bible. Neither the Hebrew Bible nor the New Testament, to say nothing of the Qur'an, is a common source material in most schools.

Yet as long as a division of labor between home and school is respected, religion courses should have a role to play in public education. Religion can be taught in the public schools as a part of the human experience and as a way for students to understand their own traditions and those of others. It is the task of the parents, should they choose, to initiate their children into a religion and to teach them to worship in a particular tradition. It is also their right to not do this. Public schools have no business in the worship business and they step over important educational and legal boundaries when they advance one religion over another or religion over nonreligion. Nevertheless, religion is a vital part of the human experience, and while many parents can engage their children in their own religious tradition, few have the knowledge or the interest to place that tradition in a wider context of traditions and interpretations, a context that we see as one of the critical dividing points between teaching religion as a devotional act and teaching it as a humanistic subject.

THE LAW AND RELIGION

Some believe that to introduce the subject of religion in public schools is unconstitutional, and hence they wrongly hold that schools cannot teach Bible or world religion without breaking the law. In fact, the Supreme Court has only ruled that devotional religious teaching is unconstitutional and has acknowledged that knowledge of religion is an important part of our intellectual heritage. The landmark 1963 Supreme Court decision, *Abington v. Schempp*, which deemed devotional reading of the Bible in public schools to be unconstitutional, had already made this quite clear.

> Nothing we have said here indicates that such study of the Bible or of religion, when presented objectively as part of a secular program of education, may not be effected consistently with the First Amendment.[9]

Indeed, as explained in the same decision, not only is religion allowed by the court:

> One's education is not complete without a study of comparative religion or the history of religion and its relationship to the advancement of civilization. It certainly may be said that the Bible is worthy of study for its literary and historic qualities.[10]

Abington did not define what would constitute an "objective" presentation of a religious subject as part of a "program in secular education." Subsequent court cases established the governing criteria, which continue to set the benchmark by which state officials and courts (whether federal or state) adjudicate the constitutionality of proposed or existing courses. The most influential of these decisions is *Lemon v. Kurtzman*, which defined a three-pronged test to determine the constitutionality of governmental action with respect to religion.[11] Although the "Lemon test" has proved controversial over the years, court challenges to public-school courses addressing topics in religious belief, practice, or literature have repeatedly been framed and adjudicated on these terms, and there is nothing about the Lemon test that prohibits schools from teaching religion courses.[12]

TEACHING *ABOUT* RELIGION

These constitutional questions aside, educational theorists have made significant contributions to the question of how to teach the subject of religion. Up to this point, we have been using the shorthand phrase to "teach religion" to refer to classroom instruction on content involving beliefs, practices, and canonical texts of religious traditions. The preferred term to refer to academic instruction, however, is to teach "about religion," terminology used by concurring justices in the *Abington* decision and prominent in both legal and educational literature since that time.[13] This distinction, it is important to note, between teaching about religion and inculcating religious beliefs and practice originated in educational, rather than legal, circles. William Vickery and Stewart Cole pointed in this direction as early as 1943, in outlining an educational model of "cultural democracy" in the United States. Religion, Vickery and Cole argued, is a "primary determinant of a people's culture," which can be "objectively considered" in terms of its sacred literature, its ritual, institutional and cultic practices, and its essential beliefs and philosophy. While not the sole determinant of culture, religion is nonetheless an important factor among the diverse forces that define a people's culture. For this reason, the authors concluded that an educator who sought to teach a realistic interpretation of American society should take account "of all the social factors"—including religion—which "have helped to shape the nature of our culture and are affecting the destiny of our people."[14]

Vickery and Cole introduced the cultural understanding of religion that would subsequently become foundational to a constitutional justification for religion as a subject in school. They did so at a time when most advocates for such courses identified the moral formation of students as the ultimate goal for religious instruction.[15] By contrast, Vickery and Cole identified the critical issue facing education as the formation of democracy in a context of cultural pluralism. "The nation's victory in the war," they warned, "will indeed be a Pyrrhic one if our race and culture attitudes prevent the kind of world co-operation we are fighting to achieve." Toward this end, the authors sought to demonstrate the need for intercultural education "to formulate a democrative philosophy of intergroup relationships."[16]

This call for a cultural approach to religion was taken up over the next two decades by a series of educational committees issuing a raft of reports and recommendations.[17] In 1947, a committee of the American Council on Education issued its manifesto, *The Relation of Religion to Public Education: The Basic Principles*, which argued for teaching about religion in a similar manner to other controversial topics, such as economics, which at the time was the hottest "culture war" issue affecting the schools. Drawing on progressive models of education, the committee established its conception of religious education as a process of guided study rather than an imparting of facts and indoctrination.[18] The committee, nevertheless, did not believe that instruction on religious subjects should be value free; it was necessary to develop a "positive attitude toward the values that religion represents in the culture."[19] This positive attitude, however, was not to be restricted to the majority traditions or the students' own traditions. The committee recommended that respect for religious diversity be a component of such a program.

All seek an increase in friendly attributes and a lessening of prejudice. There can be no progress in any of these respects except through closer acquaintanceship. We believe that this should begin as soon as students are capable of understanding the differences and will not be confused by them. It must be characterized by mutuality to the extent of a genuine desire to know one's neighbors better, to understand what they believe and why. This does not mean that a boy or girl of one faith is expected to modify his or her religious convictions. It means only that there is a will to understand.[20]

For the committee of the American Council on Education, the educational goals of guided "study of religion"—the phrase the committee preferred to "teach religion"—were several: to induce within students an appreciation for religion as both a contributing factor in American culture and a personal source of values, tolerance for and understanding of the diverse religious practices of Americans, and development of the knowledge and skills necessary for reaching reasoned assessments about religious claims.[21]

By the end of the 1940s, an outline was already developing of an educational model to constitute appropriate teaching about religion. In 1951, the Educational Policies Commission of the National Education Association (NEA) issued a report that placed its considerable stamp of approval on this general program. In addition, this commission introduced a key distinction, which would subsequently be echoed by the *Abington* court, between teaching "objectively *about* religion"—endorsed by the commission—and "advocating or teaching any religious creed."[22] (We think of this as the distinction between religious *education* in the sense of an impartial and analytic understanding on the one hand and *religious* instruction in the sense of an induction into a particular religion on the other.) The NEA, moreover, went beyond earlier commissions in identifying a further educational justification for this practice of "teaching about religion." Noting widespread ignorance of the basic practices of global religious traditions, the commission held that both the "unity of our own country" and our "understanding of other nations of the world" would be enhanced by instruction about religion in the public schools.[23] While the study about religion would not be devotional, it would not be value neutral. It would aim, rather, to deepen the "moral and spiritual values" of students and demonstrate an "attitude of friendly sympathy" toward religion. These classroom practices, it was hoped, would both promote "religious tolerance actively," and validate religion as an "important fact in our culture."[24]

These various commission reports demonstrate that well before the Supreme Court articulated its dispositive view on "objective" teaching about religion, educators had developed key principles concerning the purposes and methods for teaching "about religion" that they regarded as consistent with the duty of public schools to cultivate democratic values in American citizens.[25] They also suggest that as times and temperament vary, educational theory may continue to contribute to the national discourse about the teaching of religion.

This brief overview grounds a basic premise for this study. The courts, from *Abington* to the present, have provided, in the words of Linell E. Cady, "the judicial stamp of approval" by which the study about religion is distinguished from the profession or practice of religion.[26] The fundamental reasons, however, for "teaching about religion" rather than "teaching religion" are educational ones and consequently have legitimacy claims that are independent of judicial restrictions. To *instruct in* religion, in our usage, means to attempt to induct a child into the beliefs and practices of a specific religious group or to promote an affiliation with religion in general. To teach *about* religion means to present religion as an academic subject without attempting to sway a student's religious commitments one way or the other.[27] Since World War II, educators have consistently judged that the latter best accords not only with constitutional principles of separation of church and state, but also, more fundamentally, to the educational aims and duties of public schools. This standard has also been internalized in a number of school districts. The superintendent of one of the participating schools in our study stated flatly about the introduction of a world-religions course into the district's single high school: "For me, it was always really simple: we teach about religions, we don't teach religions. That was the line of demarcation. Kids knew, all we're talking about is *about* the religion. We will not teach you the religion. We emphasize that all the time."

PLAN OF THE BOOK

Yet as we will see in this book, what it means to "teach about religion" varies greatly from community to community, from school to school, and, most importantly for our purposes, from one type of religion course to another. As we mentioned earlier, the chapters are arranged to illustrate as they progress the liberal ideals of individual growth and civic engagement. At the outset, we should note that the names of all participating teachers, administrators, schools, organizations, and communities are pseudonymous. We have also deleted any identifying information from the statements we quote from the teachers. A more detailed description of our research method is included in the appendix. In the classes described in chapters 2 and 3, liberal ideals are overwhelmed by other aims—to compete with religious homeschooling and to maintain community support, among other purposes. In these chapters, we examine the most popular and most problematic of religion courses, Bible History. Chapter 2 examines an unusual administrative arrangement between the school and the local churches and illustrates in a most dramatic way how, in religiously conservative communities, these courses can serve to enhance the legitimacy of public schools and stem the tide to abandon them for private religious schools or homeschooling. There is a cost, however, that is paid for this effort to save public education in terms of the depth and diversity of inquiry. Chapter 3 describes the pedagogical strategies employed by religiously committed teachers, Mr. Black and Mr. Milsap, to shape a community-friendly course without *consciously* violating the court's mandates to remain neutral where matters of religion are concerned. While the teachers strive to meet religious neutrality, moral neutrality is quite a different matter. Indeed, a distinguishing mark of each of the four different kinds of courses we observed is their sense of a moral mission. In Bible History, this mission is to promote an orderly moral universe. Israel and its relation to God is presented as the moral template. The rules are clear and transparent: if you follow them, you are rewarded; break them and, just like the Israelites, you will be punished.

In chapter 4, we take up one of the primary challenges facing the Bible History format. Due to the underlying presupposition that the history of Israel illustrates an eternal moral code, Bible History courses are prone to a totalizing worldview, which in turn leaves these courses subject to either the nonrecognition of alternative views or misrecognition of outside communities and individuals. We examine the consequences of these tendencies as they emerge in the classrooms of Ridge County, and offer an alternative to resolve the dilemma one of these teachers, Mr. Black, perceives.

In chapter 5, we turn our attention from Bible History courses to a course entitled The Bible and Its Influence. This course follows the format suggested by the BLP, a national group that publishes a handsome text endorsed by a number of conservative and mainline religious (and some nonreligious) groups. Because these courses stress the influence of the Bible on culture and civilization they can more easily avoid questions about the historical truth of the Bible, and hence are on safer legal ground than most Bible History courses. Moreover, where Bible History tends toward a totalizing worldview, the Bible and its Influence strives toward equal recognition of diverse faith communities. The teacher, Mr. Watson, uses the course to enhance the student's understanding of diverse religious groups and values in the local community. While he is a committed

Christian, and draws many Christians to the elective course, he takes steps to ensure that students do not try to turn the course into a "testimonial for Jesus."

The humanities nurtures the skills required to engage with and analyze different human practices, including the disposition needed to detach oneself from a received understanding and to explore and generate alternative understandings. Chapter 6 examines the development of these skills and dispositions in a Bible as Literature class. Here, in contrast to Bible History, the Bible is treated as open, partial, and incomplete. Its message is quite different from the absolutist understanding of the moral order. Here, the Bible teachings are not an absolute, but subject for engagement and discussion.

Chapter 7 examines world-religion courses, showing how they aim to prepare students for civic engagement in a multireligious, globalized world. Here, we consider new issues. Is tolerance a legitimate goal for teachers to promote? What does it mean to respect the religious other? How far can a teacher go in challenging a student's belief? We also consider the character of moral development that is involved in engaging with the religious other.

In the final chapter, we argue that as a part of a humanities curriculum, religion courses can enhance self-reflection and encourage students to take a larger role in the shaping of their own development. We argue that this calls for a level of biblical sophistication all too rare in the courses we observed. We acknowledge the serious divide between biblical scholarship that must highlight discontinuities where they are found and high-school religion courses that are often concerned with social cohesion, tolerance, or maintaining community support. We do not propose an easy solution to this divide, but we do suggest that students would be well served if schools were to capture the sense of evolutionary dynamics that can be found within religious traditions and the ways in which different biblical writings reflect the historical concerns and responses of different religious communities to their own circumstances.

Of the Bible courses we observed, Bible as Literature courses are the most academically promising. We also believe that an understanding of world religion will be invaluable in an ever more globalizing world. However, in keeping with the liberal tradition, we hold that it is important that students be taught that the proper object of their respect is the *right* of the individual to believe, regardless of the opinion the student may hold about the truth or value of the belief.

Chapter 2

BIBLE HISTORY COURSES, I
Partnership between School and Community

Bible History courses are offered as electives by history or social-studies departments alongside of American History and World History. These courses are especially popular in rural areas in the South, but there is an effort by the National Council on Bible Curriculum in Public Schools (NCBCPS) to introduce these courses in public schools nationwide.[1] When taught in conservative Christian communities, Bible History can add to the standing of the public schools among committed Christians (and non-Christians who sympathize with the conservative moral program), serving as a counter to the growing homeschool movement and checking the expansion of Christian fundamentalist schools. By offering Bible History, the school acknowledges the importance of religion and signals its responsiveness to the values of the religious segment of the community and its partnership with the community in raising the young. This role of a Bible course is one we can describe as the "recognition" function of humanities courses. By this label, we mean that humanities courses can enable students to recognize themselves as members of the community in which they grow up, and at the same time, help schools signal that they recognize the core values of the community they inhabit. This recognition function, although basic, can serve a legitimate purpose in both the introduction and conduct of a religion course, as long as one constituency's recognition is not obtained at the nonrecognition or misrecognition of another. This chapter describes how a Bible History course can be integral to a partnership between a community and a school, while the next chapter explores the constraints on pedagogy in a Bible History course.

THE TEARVILLE BIBLE ASSOCIATION AND THE BIBLE HISTORY PROGRAM

Tearville, a racially diverse, predominantly Protestant community, is the largest city and seat of rural Tapscott County, located in a South Atlantic state. Until the last two decades, the county had relied on agriculture, textile, and furniture industries for its economic stability. The textile and furniture companies have moved away, but the proximity of Tearville to a major urban financial center has been, in the words of Benjamin Jenkins, a senior administrator for the school district, a "business engine" that has brought new manufacturing entities to the county.

The administrators at the consolidated school system of Tearville-Tapscott believe that its robust Bible History program has helped to maintain support for public education in the area. One of the notable features of its program is the Tearville Bible Association (TBA), an educational auxiliary comprised of around seventy churches in the community integrated across racial lines and drawing together a wide diversity of Protestant denominations, to support the public schools. This support has come at a time when both religious private schools and homeschooling have been outpacing the growth of the public-school population. Some district administrators credit the cooperation of the TBA for dampening a surge of interest in the county for these educational alternatives. The district's five high schools offer four "fact-based" semester-long electives on the Bible (covering the entire span of biblical literature), taught by three full-time teachers, whose salaries are covered by the TBA. Through this reciprocal arrangement between the school district and local religious communities, any interested student can select a course focused on the "Old Testament" (as the instructors and administrators invariably refer to the course) or the New Testament for every one of his or her four years of high-school study. Lester Robbins, principal of Tearville High, estimated that about 10 percent of his student body was enrolled in a Bible course every semester and that close to half of the students took at least one Bible course over a four-year period.

It would be difficult to find a more dedicated Bible program in any other public school district in the country or to find a purer example of the use of a school program to reinforce communal values. Pamela Hastings, principal of West Tapscott High School, identified the Bible course as a direct response to the community's values: "we live in the Bible Belt . . . There is a strong desire in the community for young people to have a good working knowledge of what's in the Bible." The program began in the early 1990s in response to an initiative by the TBA. According to Daniel Harding, who had served both as an administrator in the county school system and as a past president of the TBA: "it was the churches that wanted the courses in the school even though the Sunday church schools were not wanting for participants."

Certified public-school teachers teach all of the Bible courses, but the TBA pays the portion of their salary devoted to religion courses. It also donates the Bibles used in the course and subsequently retained by the students after its completion. The association also has considerable influence in the hiring of the teachers. In a two-stage hiring process, the school principal identifies a pool of qualified applicants and then a committee composed equally of school staff and TBA members conducts the interviews.[2] Many of the applicants either are ordained ministers or have theological training. The teachers, approved by the school *and* the association's representatives, develop the curriculum in consultation with the TBA, which also gives its "stamp of approval"—in the words of one of the teachers—before being submitted to the school board. The involvement of the TBA in the hiring process allows the community to ensure that Bible instructors maintain a worldview consistent with the values of the association's members. It allows the association to serve, as one teacher phrases it, as a "voice" for the community as a whole to the school system.[3]

School officials and TBA representatives provided us with a significant list of benefits they believe the Bible program has brought to the county. We were told, for example, that it has stemmed the dropout rate and encouraged creativity among less academically inclined students. Mr. Harding recalled with pride that students did an exceptional exhibit of the Last Supper, which was on prominent display in the school for other students and community members to view. The Bible course also forms a kind of social anchor for the school as the foundation to the extracurricular Bible club. This club undertakes community projects and travels to meet with other similar clubs across the state, providing, in Harding's characterization, an "extension of that classroom experience into community, into the churches." Finally, the TBA celebrates this connection between school and community with an annual banquet, in which the students pit their knowledge against local pastors in a Bible quiz. School officials claimed that the financial subsidization of the courses through the association is intended to avoid legal entanglements, but they did not explain how this financial relationship achieved this end. In other jurisdictions, private funding of Bible courses has not shielded a district from First Amendment challenge.[4] This financial structure, however, might deter parents in this district from mounting a legal challenge in the first place, even if the rationale itself is questionable.

The activities the TBA sponsors both mark for the students the importance of religion in the community's public arena and signal to the wider community the support of prestigious religious authorities for the work of the school. Indeed, the close relationship between local churches and the Tearville-Tapscott school system goes beyond the Bible History courses. Some local churches also "adopt" a nearby school, which involves, among other activities, making volunteers available for "prayer walks" and counseling of staff and students. The Bible association, in this way, represents one component of a wider pattern in the relationship between the school system and the county's churches.

The Tearville-Tapscott school district has a number of reasons to welcome the support of churches, both informally through the school "adoption" and in the formal Bible curriculum. Tearville's state has experienced considerable growth in religious, private, and home schools over the last two decades. In the 1985 school year, only 800 students in the state were reported as being homeschooled. That number had increased to over 80,000 in the 2009–10 school year, or as much as 5 percent of the total school-age population, and this official count is thought to underestimate the numbers.[5] Tapscott County itself has experienced an even sharper demographic shift than the state as a whole. The data for the 2008 school year indicates that 6.3 percent of Tearville-Tapscott children enrolled in homeschool settings, while another 5.2 percent attended private schools—that is, 11.5 percent of the total population opted out of the county's public-school system. To put these numbers in wider perspective, Tearville-Tapscott has a homeschool population that is higher than its state's average and more than twice the national average. Moreover, according to Benjamin Jenkins, chief operations officer for the district, the number of homeschoolers in his county continues to grow to the point where the local homeschool association forms an alternative school system. "They have a yearbook, they have a prom, they have field trips—things of that nature," Jenkins observed, which helps to promote a network of identity-forming relationships independent of the school as its social anchor.[6] This identity, Jenkins continues, is more religiously conservative than the general population, and these parents tend to see public school "culture" as a threat. "Folks that I have spoken to that homeschool their children," Jenkins reports, "see the public schools as a culture that they do not want to expose their children to."[7]

Still, Tearville-Tapscott officials expressed little concern that their school system was in danger of losing cultural legitimacy with its constituents and they believe that the Bible courses and the close involvement with the churches signal to the wider community that the school takes the community's religious concerns seriously. This, in turn, encourages religious members of the community to support public schools. This may not always persuade parents to opt for the public school in lieu of these other options, but it can reduce suspicion of an alien "government educating my children," as Jenkins summarizes the fears of homeschooling parents.

TEACHING FOR BIBLICAL LITERACY

The official aim of Tearville's courses is to improve biblical literacy and to help students understand the chronological order of the biblical stories. An unofficial aim is to give recognition to the community by supporting and reinforcing its values. This does not mean that the courses simply mirror the positions of the churches. Pamela Hastings, principal of West Tapscott High School at the time of our visit, served at one time as a member of a teacher-selection team. She describes her own religious affiliation as more liberally Christian than the community as a whole, but she is confident that the selection committee successfully weeded out prospective teachers who would not respect different viewpoints. While she felt that the teachers they hired were more religiously conservative than she was, she was confident that they were able to leave their own theology outside of the classroom door, and she described them as fine teachers.

David White has taught Bible in Tapscott County and other districts in the state for over twenty years. "I tend to think," White informs us, that "most of my students come from a very conservative background. And they pretty well want to look at the Bible and read what's there and take it at absolute face value." They do not want, as he tells us, to "overanalyze what's there." White is willing to tailor his teaching to meet this desire. He candidly admits, for example, that when the class gets to problematic texts: "We don't get into a real big in-depth study because some of the students study at their church and they come in with one idea and some may have other ideas. So, I guess, I just try to keep it simple.'" "Keeping it simple" and "not going into too much depth" are repeated mottos for White's teaching. He works hard to stay on the surface and believes in a pedagogy of noninterruption, where the teacher's function is to transmit information in a neutral manner. "We are basically in there," he says, "to teach the material that's there so that they have a knowledge of the events as recorded in the Bible."

Mr. White structures his class on the presumption that students already have strongly formed religious views and that the teacher should block any challenge to these views that might emerge in the classroom. Underlying this approach is a presumption that a teacher can present the Bible as a neutral "textbook" through which students can obtain transparent access to "events" as they occurred in history. Indeed, the Bible is the only "textbook" used in the class, a practice that Mr. White explains in terms of the need to preserve community harmony. It would be "impossible," he says, "to come up with a text that is harmonious in a classroom setting," because some textbooks want to discuss whether the events depicted are factual or not, and this kind of discussion could provoke discord. He tries to avoid initiating discussions of the differing interpretations that might be given to a biblical text for fear that this would challenge the students' understanding of the character of the text.

In engaging in the seemingly bland and straightforward process of transmitting "fact," Mr. White legitimates his own teaching practice by appealing to a vision of the teacher as a neutral conveyor of information. At the same time, he shields the subject matter from further interrogation by students: one can either accept a "fact" or not; it is not something that admits to further questioning. For his churchgoing Christian students, his shielding of the subject matter from critical interrogation and his resistance to "overanalysis" subordinate the teaching activity of the school to the interpretive authority of the churches. Mr. White's pedagogy of noninterruption also aligns well with the relationship between school and community as structured in the cooperation of the system with the Bible association. The TBA supports the school by funding these courses, while the school supports the community by providing the scaffolding of "facts" upon which the church will then superimpose the applied "meaning."

We should add here that Mr. White does not present this naïve conception as his own view of the Bible. He demonstrates awareness of alternative traditions of biblical reading and also of contemporary scholarship on at least some issues. For example, Mr. White is aware of the threefold division of the Hebrew

Scriptures in Jewish tradition and of historically oriented scholarship on the Book of Revelation. Such knowledge, however, does not become part of the classroom culture unless the students seek it from him. Although he is aware of ample material in the Bible to provoke moral or intellectual questions, Mr. White's policy is to answer questions if and only if the students raise them. Difficult questions, however, rarely arise spontaneously, and White describes his don't ask, don't tell policy with a self-deprecating laugh: "we just sort of stick to the text the way it is," he explains, "and if those questions don't come up, then I don't deal with them." In other words, Mr. White takes it for granted that the "very conservative view of the Bible"—which is his description—of his students should be allowed to stand, and that his approach to teaching should take into account that the students also study the Bible in their various church settings. The teacher strives to not insert himself between the students and their experiences outside of the classroom.

Mr. White's pedagogy of noninterruption is not intended to promote dialogue, but rather to inhibit inquiry and to allow dominant preunderstandings to remain undisturbed. Tearville's educators like Mr. White go beyond the course's function as means to recognize *the* community. In using the Bible courses to *mirror* the community, the school also serves to define what that "community" is. It is significant that Mr. White regards as a key component of the job to assure that the students take the Bible at face value and avoid "overanalyzing" it. In his mind, he is honoring the wishes of the parents and the students and is neither advancing nor discouraging—to echo constitutional language—a religious view. He is simply providing students with information and by doing so, allowing everything to remain unchanged. That most of the students finish the course believing the same things that they did when they entered is taken as a sign of success. It leaves everything as is, including the students' purported desire to "not overanalyze" the Bible.

THE PROBLEMS OF A PEDAGOGY OF NONINTERRUPTION

As important as it is to recognize the local experience, there is more to education than transmission of local culture and reinforcing local values. In a good humanities course, if students do not want to analyze the text, teachers will encourage them to do so. To report that students are not interested in analyzing the Bible is much more than a description of a given state of affairs, even if accurate. It is also a statement about the goals of teaching Bible at Tearville: stay on the surface and discourage critical engagement by practicing a pedagogy of noninterruption.

Some valuable opportunities are missed because of this aim. For example, students might have been asked to compare the two accounts of creation in Genesis 1 and 2. Modern critical scholarship has indeed employed the variation between the two accounts to support the well-known source theory of the "documentary hypothesis."[8] Nevertheless, students could gain much from a comparison of Genesis 1 and 2 without endorsing critical theories. Or they could have been asked to closely examine the Exodus story and discuss the reasons why Pharaoh kept reversing his own decision whether to let the Israelites go. This topic could be approached either on the basis of multiple sources or from a perspective of ethical reasoning—our point is that these literary exercises can be undertaken without posing a challenge to the student's received doctrine of biblical inspiration.

Given these and other exciting possibilities, it takes considerable effort simply to remain on the surface and not to engage in analysis. We will look at some of the techniques for achieving the goal of limiting instruction to surface transmission in the next chapter. For now, it is sufficient to point out that while recognition is certainly one of the functions of the humanities, recognition without interpretation is a very blunt instrument. To explore this intentional myopia, let's return briefly to look at the demographic makeup of Tearville and the changes that are occurring.

Tearville, as noted earlier, is the largest city and seat of rural Tapscott County. The gradual absorption of Tearville into a wider urban region reduced some of the dominance of the white Protestant population, as the Hispanic Catholic population has increased and as the prominence of international financial interests has attracted a small number of other ethnic and religious groups, including Muslims, to the region. The Bible program has not kept pace with this diversification. It is telling that in our interview Mr. White can recall his single self-identified Jewish student over his twenty years of experience. Indeed, groups such as the Rotary Club have declined to participate in the Bible program out of concern that not all religious points of view are represented.

The reluctance of the Rotary Club to participate highlights a concern about religion in the public schools and the difficulty of representing all points of view. What often passes as communal authority is more precisely the voice of one segment—often the most vocal, if not the most interested—rather than the full spectrum of the community. This need not always be a problem. Providing special recognition to the experience of local people is often a sound educational principle, but determining what *counts* as the "local people" is not always easy in a mobile, pluralistic society. Public schools, consequently, must be concerned that in recognizing one segment of a community they do not misrecognize, or fail to recognize, another. These twin dangers of nonrecognition and misrecognition are the primary risks that beset programs such as Tearville-Tapscott's: in emphasizing the dominant local tradition they either neglect the legitimate traditions and viewpoints of less visible minorities (nonrecognition) or they represent a minority's tradition solely through the perspective of the dominant majority (misrecognition). We take up these pitfalls more fully in chapter 4, but let us provide a brief illustration in terms of a Bible course. A Bible curriculum that divides its courses between "Old Testament" [*sic*] and "New Testament" falls prey to misrecognition in that it institutionalizes a structure that presents the Jewish Bible in terms of its Christian reception. A course that treats the Christian canonical "Old Testament" without mention of the corpus of deuterocanonical writings—those added to the Hebrew Bible in the subsequent Greek-language translations and received as canonical within large segments of the Christian community—can be criticized for nonrecognition, in that it fails to bring to attention the diversity of the biblical canons within Christianity itself.

These examples of misrecognition and nonrecognition are minor and belong among the class of professional missteps rather than constitutional liabilities. Our point is that an approach to religion within a humanities framework must be mindful of the broad aim of initiating students into a public. The construction of a democratic public requires two things. First, it requires equal recognition among groups. Second, it requires openness in terms of what groups to define as part of the community. This is what we call the "welcoming function" of a public school, where it must provide a hospitable environment for members of groups that may not yet be physically represented in the local community. A noneducational example would be the now illegal real-estate covenants that would otherwise restrict the selling of homes to a certain religious or racial group not yet present as homeowners.

Tearville educators realize that their students are already entwined with a specific cultural identity that bears certain religious markers. As Mr. White makes clear to us, it is his policy to respect this identity by allowing it to stand without interruption—a form, we would say, of implicit recognition. They believe that recognition is achieved without misrecognition or nonrecognition of others because the courses are electives and not required. Hence, nonbelievers and members of other religious groups are not required to attend courses that are intended to deal with the origins of the Christian faith in both the "Old" and the New Testaments. Yet whether this benign view of recognition is accurate depends on what happens inside the classrooms of Tearville and other schools like it. For a closer look at this aspect of recognition, we turn from the macro view of the administrative arrangement at Tearville and enter the micro view of the classroom at the schools of Ridge County.

Chapter 3

BIBLE HISTORY COURSES, II
The Art of Staying on the Surface

David White, as discussed in the previous chapter, advocates a pedagogy of presenting the text at face value, avoiding "overanalysis," and staying on the surface. By staying on the surface, Bible History courses in communities like Tearville legitimize the public school and gain the support of Christian parents and parents who wish to affirm the authority of a traditional Protestant worldview even if they do not identify as practicing members of a church.[1] Staying on the surface, however, is not always as easy as it sounds, given a group of potentially curious adolescents, many of whom care about God and religion and who, if left to their own devices, could ask difficult and probing questions.[2] Staying on the surface is an art requiring considerable pedagogical skill—the kind of knowledge of one's craft that can take years to develop. Morris Black, a highly respected teacher in Ridge County, a religiously conservative community much like Tearville-Tapscott, illustrates this art.

With only a one-semester course in the Old Testament [*sic*], the Bible program in Ridge County is not nearly as extensive as that in Tearville. Nevertheless, the communities are similar in many ways and have much in common religiously, although Ridge's population is poorer, whiter, and less socially mobile than that of Tearville. In the year 2000, less than 5 percent of the population of Ridge County had graduated from a four-year college.

The Bible History course in Ridge originated after a local grassroots advocate approached the school board with the request to develop a new Bible elective. The board approved the idea, but instead of working with local clergy, the board turned over the development of the prospective course to the principal at Ridge County High School. The district was thus responsive to community concerns, but unlike Tearville-Tapscott, it vetted the course and teachers in more traditional ways. Thus, the community churches neither have a direct role in the hiring of Bible teachers nor do they contribute to their salary.

The two Bible teachers, Mr. Morris Black and Mr. Aaron Milsap, are members of their schools' history departments; they take history seriously and use it both to transmit a clearer understanding of events depicted in the Bible and to enlarge their students' understanding of their own times. Both teachers are committed to transmitting—or at least not disrupting—the religious beliefs and values of their students or the community. They are conscious of the limitations that the First Amendment places on their teaching and they take care not to violate these limits intentionally. Moreover, they wish to respect parental rights to guide the religious education of their children and they try to respect the autonomy of their students. The default position is not to disrupt, and, wherever possible, to reinforce the prevalent religious orientation of the community.

THE PEDAGOGY OF COMMUNITY RECOGNITION

Morris Black introduced Bible History at Ridge High School in January 2000. He has taught the course two quarters each year since then, and in the fall of 2007, his colleague, Aaron Milsap, brought the course to the newly opened Northridge High School. Milsap intentionally follows the curriculum developed by Black, so that the courses should have an identical structure despite the different settings. More recently, other counties in the same state have approached Ridge to use Black's curriculum as a model. The course covers the history of Israel from Abraham (Genesis 12) to the end of the reign of Solomon (1 Kings 11), and establishes as its primary aim the chronological reconstruction of the events referred to in the biblical books that address this time period. Black had originally designed this syllabus as "Bible History I," and intended to extend the curriculum to complete the rest of Old Testament [sic] history in Bible History II. Due, however, to the administrative needs of the school, Black has not been able to offer the companion course and he feels that the trajectory of the history is somewhat truncated by the constraints on the curriculum.

The rubric "Bible History" can cover a lot of ground and can communicate

a range of signals to the community. The Tearville-Tapscott school district selected the history rubric as a means to signal that the course was not a "devotional religion class." Mr. Black also told us that defining the course as "history"
sends a reassuring signal to the legal as well as to the nonreligious segment of
the community.

> Our major concern, I suppose, in the very beginning was to reassure stu-
> dents and parents that this was a history course and that it wasn't any kind of
> devotional-type situation. It was non-proselytizing and that it was set up like a
> history course and taught like a history course. And that it *was* a history course.

Teachers and administrators in both school districts explain that the designation of the course as "history" strikes the note of legal permissibility—that is,
one that truly "academic" courses carry. But the designation of "Bible History"
also communicates something else to the conservative Christian members of
this community. It signals that the Bible itself will be treated as a primary historical text that can serve to reconstruct a reliable history of world events in
general and of Israel in particular. This reading works to reassure evangelicals
in the community, as it suggests that the course will not seek to undermine the
faith basis of the students and might even reinforce it by lending to the Bible the
sanction that inclusion in a *public*-school curriculum provides.

There is another possible conception of history that belongs more distinctively to biblical scholars. In biblical scholarship, historical research aims to reconstruct the political, social, and cultural contexts in which the producers and
original recipients of biblical texts lived, and in this effort to facilitate a more
precise understanding of the worldviews of these authors and readers.[3] This
is far distant from Black's usage of the term. He does not perceive a need to
contextualize the events reported in the biblical narratives by reference to the
sources through which the modern reader gains knowledge of them. As we will
see later, this contributes to a particular dilemma Black faces in joining together
his conception of history as an academic discipline with the moral order he
discerns in biblical history.

Framing the course by approaching the Bible as a historical source can invite legal challenge. In 1997, a federal judge in Florida upheld a challenge to one
district's Bible courses, in part due to the presentation of the resurrection as a
historical fact.[4] The previous year in Mississippi, another federal judge deemed

that teaching the Bible as a "historical text" in the sense of "as events that actually happened" could be construed as indicating a motive for the class as imparting religious doctrine.[5] The limits of what can be taught as "history" in "Bible History" are also on the mind of the administrators of Tearville-Tapscott. Pamela Hastings, principal of West Tapscott High, acknowledged to us that she was uncomfortable with a blanket approach to teaching all the biblical narratives equally as "history." When she interviewed prospective teachers, Hastings told us, she asked them about how they would approach the Eden story—whether or not they would represent the early chapters of Genesis without qualification as "literal truth."

> If they're going to teach that as the literal truth, Adam and Eve, the whole bit, then they're teaching that as history. And we honestly don't know; there's no way for us to know for sure. And so, I just have a very strong personal interest in making sure that it is [not] used as history.

Ms. Hastings raises concerns with teaching the opening chapters of Genesis as "literal truth" because of the empirical uncertainty, "there's no way for us to know for sure." Consequently, she believes it wise for teachers to avoid placing themselves in a position of having to make a firm judgment on the historical accuracy of the narratives.

We don't know the grounds on which Hastings insisted on this reservation, whether pedagogical or legal. Some courts have indeed held that teaching the creation narratives as "literal truth" can be adduced as evidence of transgressing constitutional lines of religious neutrality.[6] Both Black and Milsap have a keen awareness of the susceptibility to constitutional challenge and work hard to avoid it. Morris Black designed the course to begin with the Abraham narrative in Genesis 12 and extending to the end of the reign of Solomon (1 Kings 11:44). As a result, this course detaches the area that is most likely to arouse controversy about historical accuracy—that is, the creation stories in Genesis. Since the ancestral and national narratives are not culturally contested points (although scholars have frequently questioned the historicity of these narratives) in the same way as creation and evolution, the concept of Bible as "history" can be allowed to develop without provoking the same level of scrutiny. Moreover, for students who are committed to a literal-historical conception of the first chapters of Genesis, the treatment of the *rest* of the biblical narrative in these terms implicitly supports that view without forcing it to a question.

Mr. Black teaches American history as well as Bible history, and, as we will see, has a strong sense of his academic responsibility to the discipline of history and values it for the perspective that students can gain from it. He frequently makes connections between events as reported in the "Old Testament" and contemporary happenings in the personal lives of the students as well as in the world at large. He wants them to develop perspective, see patterns, and learn to connect acts to their consequences. When the course is complete, no student need ask: why do we study history? While Morris Black's delivery is slow and methodical and his wit is dry, his message is a powerful one: history has a lesson for you!

He understands the course to be an academic history elective on a par with any other humanities elective. The course is, he tells us, "just like any other history course." Black explains: "I think the students are challenged to not just think about these people as names in a book, but see what battles they had to fight because of who they thought they were." Although students might feel a more natural connection with events in American history, Black believes the events narrated in the Bible have a continuing impact on their lives: "just because something happened three thousand years ago it doesn't mean that it still doesn't affect you. It affects the choices you make, and the things that you believe in, and the way you go about your business, just the same as U.S. history does."

In contrast to Tearville, where there were four separate electives and where courses in both "Old" and New Testament were available, Black is somewhat handicapped. His class is but a one-semester elective in the "Old Testament" as the history of the people of Israel. Nevertheless, it is jam-packed with information, and students are expected to learn many facts. Yet we should not think of the course as just the place where information is transmitted from Black to the students. Black has a view of history as a moral unfolding. As he puts it to his students:

> God will dwell among them [sc. Israel], give them guidance, give them counsel, give them advice, but it all hinges on their obedience. Obeying Moses, obeying the Ten Commandments, obeying the Levitical law. . . . In other words, God's telling them, "You do things my way and I've got your back." . . . So there are

rewards if they obey, but there is punishment if they disobey—The people are told if they disobey and they have some of this stuff happen—sudden terror, enemies coming up, wild beasts—if the people come back and say, "You know what, we really goofed, we really made a big mistake, our bad," then God would forgive them, and he would remember the covenant, and they would be restored back to the way it was before they disobeyed. So, that is the belief on the part of the Israelites. If we do good, we get good; if we do bad, bad things will happen. If we slip up and do bad, we can come back. There's a way back.

Black, as we will see more in what follows, has a clear sense of the moral code that the Bible should convey. He feels constrained, however, by the discipline of history to present that moral vision as mediated through the historical experience of Israel. Let us now turn to how he resolves this dilemma.

TEACHING THE BIBLE IN THE DISCIPLINE OF HISTORY: THE TRANSMISSION OF A METANARRATIVE

Mr. Black is a serious, no-nonsense, but friendly teacher with a wry sense of humor, who largely lectures to his class of about twenty students. He wants his students to take the Bible seriously as history, but he does not want to do anything that might upset their established beliefs. Nevertheless he is aware of the constitutional restrictions and tells us, "I know that this can't be a religious course. I mean, it can't even be perceived as religion." He makes that same point emphatically to his students in his introductory overview.

> It is a history course and it deals with biblical people, mostly people mentioned in the Old Testament of the Bible and most of the time it's talking about the Israelites. . . . What is NOT this course? It is NOT devotional time. We can't take and go to the other side of the football field and have devotion, that kind of thing. It is not overseen by a church. There is no one church, there is no church that's telling us what to say, telling us how to teach this course. Bottom line: it's a history course.

What does it mean to define this as a "history course"? For Black, it means primarily one thing: to establish the chronological succession of events as reported in the Bible. This endeavor requires, Black tells his students, exhaustive attention to detail.

> The thing about studying the Bible, the Old Testament, you got to be careful. If you leave anything out, you'll read something in a later book and it will say something like about the Edomites, and you'll go "Who are these people?" Well, those people are linked all the way back to Esau. See, there's many links, that if you leave out a link, you lose a lot of information, a lot of valuable information. So, it's very hard to study the Old Testament and to know what to leave out and what to not leave out. So, we're trying to hit all the important facts as much as we can.

Being able to identify the Edomites might not seem initially to be a crucial piece of information, but Mr. Black is convinced that the links are intricate, overlapping, and indispensable. As an example, he immediately follows this warning about forgetting the Edomites with an example he finds directly relevant: the story of Judah's siring of children by his daughter-in-law, Tamar.

> This is an example of what I'm talking about when you're talking about a link. Because what happens here, what happens with Judah and his daughter-in-law, Tamar, there is a link, there is a family lineage that comes out of this, that is linked according to the Bible all the way down to the family of Jesus. All the way down to Jesus himself. All the way down to the New Testament. So this is what I'm talking about. If you leave stuff out, there's just going to be big gaps in your mind of what's going on.

This digression is an intriguing aside in Black's lesson. He seeks to impress a methodological point about Bible study upon his students: that it is difficult to know in advance what information will be significant and what information will have limited relevance. It is telling, however, that the reference point for what is "significant" is provided by Tamar's role as one of the four women to receive mention in the gospel of Matthew's genealogy of Jesus (cf. Matthew 1:3). Black doesn't dwell on or expand on the lineage of Jesus—he is not seeking here to "prove" the messianic descent of Jesus. The ultimate fulfillment of Israel's history in Jesus is taken for granted; it need not be demonstrated in the classroom. Black instead leverages this shared cultural point to secure his students' assent on the need to conduct the class as a thorough and minute reconstruction of the events they will encounter in the Bible.

Mr. Black advances, sometimes explicitly, often implicitly, both a literal and linear reading of the Bible. His text, *The Chronological Bible*, purports to puts biblical events in the proper order.[7] Black emphasizes the significance of this choice of text in his introductory lecture.

> "Chronological" means that we are covering this course according to time. And it's going to stay in sequence—the things that happen are going to be in sequence. See the problem with studying the Bible as a Bible student is that the Bible is not in order, if you've ever noticed. The Old Testament is not really laid out in chronological—*some of it* is laid out in chronological order, but not all of it is. But I have found a book that gives the Old Testament in chronological order. And so if you want to bring your own Bible you can. If you've got a Bible, you don't have to have one. But that's what we're going to use as our textbook is everybody is going to use this book and that way we're all on a level playing field. Everybody's going to have access to the same information in the same order.

The use of a chronological Bible has little direct impact on the actual sequence of lessons in Black's class. Nevertheless, the concept of the chronological Bible reinforces the view that the Bible conveys events that can confidently be aligned in a particular time and place.

The selection of the text and the framing of the course mark the first step in his metanarrative of this Bible History course: the conveying of the unspoken message that the Bible provides a reliable and transparent window to formative events of the ancient past that still resonate in the contemporary world. The object of the course supports this framing. The aim of the class is simply to define the correct *sequence* of events. It is not to investigate the questions that one might raise with respect to a narrative. Inquiries that do not advance the reconstruction of a linear historical sequence are not initiated by Black and students are quietly discouraged from pursuing them. For Mr. Black, the events as described in the Bible are unquestionable facts and not really open to analysis or critical discussion. He will, however, often raise rhetorical questions to address a gap in the narrative, and on the very rare occasion when a student raises a question, Black will allow that some details have been left out of the story. The effect is to cut off most critical inquiry that might occur.

An example of this arises when the teacher presents a detailed rehearsal of the story of the rape of Jacob's daughter, Dinah, by a character named Shechem

(Genesis 34). Black tells the class that Jacob's sons set up a ruse to exact revenge for this outrage against their sister: they pretended to agree to allow Dinah to marry Shechem in exchange for all the men of the village (which was also named Shechem) undergoing circumcision. While the men were recuperating from the circumcision, the narrative continues, two of Dinah's brothers killed all the men of the village. At this point, Black feels that he has covered the material and picks up the narrative with Jacob's continued journeys after the slaughter at Shechem. One student, however, wants to linger on this account, and what ensues is one of the most extensive exchanges between teacher and student in the entire term of the course.

> STUDENT: Like maybe so they attacked them? Was that like they were circumcised and they were going with them? Like they were going with them on the journey or they were there in the city, and they attacked them and killed those guys?
>
> BLACK: They just attacked the men in their city after they were trying to recover from—
>
> STUDENT: Just those people that were circumcised?
>
> BLACK: Yes
>
> STUDENT: Even the one guy that she married?
>
> BLACK: Yes. Yeah. Yeah, that's my understanding. I don't know exactly how many were killed or wounded or whatever from that, but that's, but it was an attack on the men of that city because all of the men had to be circumcised of that city, according to the agreement that Jacob worked out.

Black ends the colloquy at this point to resume the thread of Jacob's travels through Canaan. The student's initial question is not entirely clear, but Black does not probe it. The student may simply be seeking clarification on the extent of the action against the Shechemites, but the follow-up questions may point to another area of interest. The student may be flagging a question of the proportionality of the response by Jacob's sons to the offense against their sister, whether murder is a just recompense for rape, or whether all the men of the town justly suffer the same fate as the one who committed the original offense, or whether the betrothal should exempt Shechem from the assault. At any rate, some adventurous teachers might employ the biblical narrative at this point to help the student probe those questions, but Black's concern with itemizing the sequence of events blunts that and other possible avenues of inquiry. He admits to his student that one cannot securely and precisely identify the body count, but this admission of a gap in the narrative also deflects any deeper questions.

Ironically, although he thinks of the Bible as a moral exemplar, Black's approach to Bible History blunts inquiry into the moral assessment of the actions taken by the Israelites, whether it be the slaughter of the Shechemites, or, later in the semester, the annihilation of the Amalekites as ordered by God (1 Samuel 15:1–33). Black also systematically preempts questions that might open up room to probe the accuracy of the biblical narrative. Staying on the surface entails anticipating potential problems and responding to them before they arise, as illustrated in the following excerpt from his lecture on Abraham.

> Abraham dies but not until he's 175. 175 years old, Abraham dies, according to the Bible. And again, people ask how did these people live so long? Well, you know what, they didn't have air pollution. They didn't have water pollution. You know the ozone layer was in pretty good shape four thousand years ago. They didn't mess up their world kind of like we have. The rainforests were in pretty good shape. There wasn't as many diseases in the world. There's been a lot of explanations, but you know by and large it was a healthier lifestyle. Fewer carbohydrates.

Black drops in the last two words with his patented understated sense of humor. More substantively, he anticipates an obvious objection to the utility of the Bible as a historical account. "People ask," he says, "how did these people live so long?" He does not wait for a student to raise the question; nor does he wait for a student to address it. Rather, he maintains the surface by blocking discussion and offering up an apologetic response. This approach not only affirms the truth of the biblical narrative, it also leaves standing the attitude of some fundamentalists that the Bible should not be questioned in a critical way.

FRAMING BY BLOCKING

In the example just mentioned, we described Black's technique of rhetorical questioning as a form of "blocking." We refer by that term to a strategy of classroom management often used by teachers to avoid a distracting side topic or to maintain a focus. "Let's hold off on that issue" or "we could go into that topic, but let's not" would be explicit verbal blocks. Eye contact can be a nonverbal method of blocking, as teachers tacitly acknowledge students who are prone to ask acceptable questions while ignoring those whose questions are likely to be off the mark. In Black's case, blocking involves, among other things, anticipating a problematic issue, then posing a rhetorical question related to that issue, and dismissing it before the students have a chance to ask (or answer) it. We could, for example, consider how the age of Abraham might have emerged in a different kind of classroom. Another teacher might have adduced the numerous archeological studies that document the age at death, on the basis of exhumed human remains, as much lower in premodern eras than our own. On that basis, the teacher might have raised for classroom discussion what explanations students might offer for the apparent discrepancy between the assigned ages of the biblical patriarchs and matriarchs and the archeological evidence. This kind of investigative exercise makes Black extremely nervous. He admits to us that he should promote more discussion but is concerned lest he is not able to control its direction. For example, had he encouraged questions about the age of the patriarchs it might have raised as an explicit topic of classroom discussion the authority of the Bible as a witness to historical events.

We approached this issue in one of our interviews with Mr. Black. In a class on King Saul, Black arrived at the theologically problematic narrative of Saul's visit to the medium (translated in traditional versions as "witch") of Endor to ask her to contact the prophet Samuel from beyond the grave (1 Samuel 28). In this narrative, the medium successfully raises the prophet, who then predicts the death of Saul and his sons in an upcoming conflict with the Philistines. The narrative is potentially problematic for believers for several reasons. First, Saul's visit to a medium other than one directly instituted by God could be viewed as a violation of specific commandments in biblical law. Second, it suggests that a person can access supernatural powers independently of God's approval. Finally, it might be disturbing to a devout reader that the prophet Samuel, a holy man, is presented as subject to the magical powers of a nonbeliever. In class, Black "blocked" the issue, rhetorically questioning the nature of the event as described, and then offering an array of possible explanations, including that the king was deluded into believing that he encountered the risen Samuel. Black concluded the sequence without asking students to respond or providing an opportunity for them to do so. The next day we asked him about his reasoning for this approach to the narrative. He explained it to us by reference to the mixed nature of his classroom.

> There might be some students in there that are believers sitting right by nonbe-lievers. What if they think the Bible is baloney and they're not believing, and, you know, they don't, because you might be sitting next to a Christian person or a Jewish person and they're thinking "Well, God gave the witch this power to be able to call up Samuel," but there's many other people that practice secret arts in the Old Testament as well. It's not just this one isolated person. So, how did they get their power? You've just got to keep an open—you don't want to shut out a nonbeliever. You've got to give them some room to be able to identify with these people in the Bible and give them room for explanations and things.

The fear that Mr. Black expresses here is that certain narratives might prompt a nonbeliever to dismiss the narrative of the Bible as a real history. Yet the explanation that the nonbeliever might offer, or the questions he or she might raise, remains private. Questions about God or God's powers are blocked from arising.

The technique of blocking provides Black with multiple benefits. It reassures devout students that rational explanations are possible for points that may seem perplexing to them and it models how they might develop a manageable answer to these thorny questions. At the same time, it allows him to include nonbelieving students within the instructional framework of the class by reference to nonsupernatural explanations for events that seem to presume a supernatural cause. Most subtly, blocking establishes implicit guidelines for what is counted as acceptable discourse, sending a sotto voce message that questioning the authority of the biblical history is an avenue that meets a dead end.

It takes considerable pedagogical skill to deliver this message without violating constitutional limits. The problem for Black is this: what pedagogical practice can sustain (or at least avoid undermining) the historical authority of the Bible while adhering to constitutional principles, at least as he perceives them? To put the question another way: how might a teacher deliver in a constitutionally acceptable way the metanarrative that the stories are a historically accurate depiction of the relation of the people of Israel to God and of God's moral plan for nations?

FRAMING THE NARRATIVE:
THE MIRACLE DISCLAIMER

At our initial interview, Mr. Black walked us through his introductory Pow-erPoint presentation and called our attention to a particular slide alerting students that they will encounter in the biblical narratives different, and potentially alienating, events and customs. Some of these customs include polygamy and violent subjugation of enemy peoples. Black explains that they should be prepared for this type of material, but also that they should suspend judgment in light of a moral and cultural system quite different from their own.

Listed among the types of narratives that students might find problematic are events, Black says, that the Bible "describes" as "miraculous."[8] He explained to us that he includes miracle narratives in his list of standard cautions in response to a First Amendment–training workshop that he attended. The leaders of the workshop, he says, advised him explicitly to inform students that they were free to offer a variant explanation for miracles and that this will not affect their grade. This is what we call the "miracle disclaimer." Black described to us the miracle disclaimer in the following way.

> I explain to the kids if you have another explanation and you want to explain it, you are free to do that. But that they're going to hear the *biblical* version of it, and then, if they choose, they don't have to make a decision if they choose to believe that or not. It's not, "do you accept this, or do you not?" It's just "this is the historical record of these people" and whatever they take from that, however they want to explain that in their mind, they're free to do that.[9]

The specific example Black provides of such an event is the parting of the sea in Exodus 14. As Black understands the constitutional requirement, he must not coerce students into believing that the parting of the sea was a "miraculous" event. At the same time, he feels it constitutionally safe to define the parting of the sea as a "historical event" which the "biblical version" presents as miraculous.[10]

Black's actual presentation of the miracle disclaimer to his students corresponds generally to his explanation to us, but with a few interesting divergences. We'll quote the entirety of his comments in the lecture on this point.

There are things referred to as miracles in the Bible. In other words, there are things described in the Bible that could only have happened if some sort of higher being had intervened and made it happen. In other words, things that defy the laws of nature—like when the Red Sea parts. That's not something that just happens every day. But a lot of people have trouble studying the Bible because of miraculous things that are described. And if you fit into that category, that's fine. If you've got a way to explain something in your mind—like if you have an explanation for how the Red Sea opened, and you want that to be your explanation, that's fine. There's not going to be any points taken off if you don't believe the miraculous things that happened. This course is not intentionally designed to make believers out of nonbelievers. OK? It's intended to be informative. It's a history course. So does anybody have any questions on that? [Brief Pause]. I kind of feel like Forrest Gump—that's all I have to say about that. OK? At least right now. OK? [Longer Pause] OK? Anybody? [Brief Pause]

No students take up this invitation to question or discuss the issue. In his private explanation to us, Mr. Black had emphasized the role of legal authority in motivating his insertion of the "miracle disclaimer" into his lecture. In the classroom presentation he allows the legal authority to remain in the background; he does not alert the students to his view that miracle narratives manifest a constitutional line between "history" and "religion." At the same time, he fleshes out what it is about miracles that brings that line into play for him. He proffers the position that miraculous occurrences, absent some naturalizing explanation, constitute a demonstration of the existence of a divine being. Therefore, accepting a miracle qua miracle would, in Black's view, support religious belief, and compelling a student to accept this proposition would constitute for him an abridgment of the student's freedom of conscience. This is the line that his class cannot cross. While in our interview Black defined the disclaimer in terms of constitutional legitimacy, in this classroom presentation he adopts the language of educational legitimacy: "This course is not intentionally designed to make believers out of nonbelievers . . . It's intended to be informative. It's a history course." The disciplinary boundary of history now becomes the basis for the disclaimer.

Black appeals to disciplinary constraints as the basis for creating a private space for individual conscience within the classroom. At the same time, *he* uses those disciplinary constraints to shield the miracle narratives from inquiry. In our interview, Black had proposed that students retained freedom to explain miracles alternatively either in their own minds *or* by raising the issue for the classroom *as a whole*.

> So, instead of saying "This happened this way," that's why I say "Most Jews and Christians believe this" and that gives them the opportunity in their mind to say "Well,"—or even to say out loud—"well, I'm not going to believe it. I choose not to believe that." And if they say it silently, that's fine; if they want to say it out loud, just as long as they do not disturb the class—or *disrupt* the class—they may disturb the class with what they say, not to be disruptive, not just to yell something out just to get attention.

Black's statement seems at first to open a wider space for doubt to enter the classroom, but this extension of permission from the individual to the classroom as a whole is tentative at best. His phrasing that "Most Jews and Christians believe this" might obliquely provide the "opportunity"—to use Black's word—but this does not constitute an invitation for them to undertake a joint examination of the issue. Moreover, to the extent that students identify with either of the two confessional communities, this form of demarcating a religious boundary deters individual students from probing too deeply. Black does not invite students to raise their doubts vocally, but instead simply permits them their mental reservations.

Finally, when Black presents to the students the Exodus narrative itself, the "miracle disclaimer" is not mentioned at all. Black paints a vivid picture of the flight of the Israelites from the pursuing Egyptian army.

> Then the people see that Pharaoh's army is coming. And they've got the Red Sea on one side, they've got Pharaoh's army on the other side, and they start complaining—why couldn't we just have died in Egypt? And then you have the miracle of all miracles. Moses lifts his staff and the Red Sea parts, and a million plus people cross over. The Bible says "on dry land"—the Red Sea stayed open all night long. Kind of like Walmart, stayed open all night. They left Egypt, they crossed over the Red Sea—the Bible says on dry land—they came over to the other side, and the Egyptian army was in pursuit, but when they came through the middle of the sea, they were in the process of crossing over on dry land, but the Bible says, the waters closed up on the Egyptians and they perished in the sea.

In this lecture, Mr. Black describes this event without qualification as the "miracle of all miracles." He does not repeat the miracle disclaimer, nor does he pause to ask (as he frequently does in other circumstances) if the students have any questions. The "miracle disclaimer" then functions as a generic caution at the outset of the course, but is not integrated into the fabric of the class. By permitting students at the outset of the term privately to hold their own reservations, but by discouraging students from raising them vocally, Mr. Black inoculates the class as a whole from undertaking this potentially unsettling exploration. As a consequence, the disclaimer, while permitting a certain degree of freedom to the student, also constrains the scope of inquiry. Students are, Black carefully explains to us, permitted to entertain alternative *explanations* of the parting of the sea, but he does not extend that permission to questioning whether the purported parting of the sea occurred at all.[11]

Black wants to communicate more than simply the stories related by the Bible. He also wants to transmit and mark as correct an important metanarrative—the Bible is a real and literal history of God's relation to the Israelite nation, and it reveals God's plans for individuals and nations. Goodness involves following those plans. Badness involves disobeying them. Thus, the "biblical version" provides a "historical record" of the Israelites, and the only appropriate correction is one of chronology. This metanarrative is rarely expressed directly to the students, but it is a message that is delivered through the pedagogy itself—by what is said and what is not said, and by what is marked as important or ignored as unimportant. In his lecture, Black signals to the students that questions might be raised about the accuracy or completeness of the biblical version as a historical account, but in the same breath he blocks further discussion.

> Now a lot of people will say, "well, why is this not in Egyptian history? Why don't they record this?" The truth of the matter is that Egyptian pharaohs did not record defeats in their history. Because they wanted to go down, kind of like the coach wants to go down undefeated. In order to do that, they did not record any of their losses. So you'll have a hard time finding that in Egyptian history, or any other Egyptian loss that they sustained.

In this blocking maneuver, Black acknowledges the possibility for doubt but in doing so quells any incipient challenge to the status of the biblical narrative as a historical record. The effect of narrow and ambivalent usage of the miracle disclaimer is to block more challenging probing of the conception of the Bible as a "historical" book. We'll provide one more example for consideration: Black's presentation of the story of Abraham and Isaac (Genesis 22). He establishes it as a real event and blocks from consideration any one of the many rich ways in which the story has been appropriated for its theological significance. Mr. Black comes to the end of the story of the interrupted sacrifice of Isaac by his father, Abraham.

> They go up to the top of the mountain and according to the Bible, many Jews and Christians believe, that before Abraham actually kills Isaac he is stopped. Abraham is stopped by—someone intervenes. Again, is it an angel, is it a man of God, is it a mirage in the desert? I don't have any way of explaining these things. A lot of people wonder how old was Isaac when that happens? And see the Bible doesn't exactly tell on that. You can do a little deducing, but you can't pinpoint it down. [A] lot of people put Isaac as a young boy, six, eight, ten years old. Some other people put him as like eighteen, twenty, twenty-two, maybe even twenty-five years old. It's not real clear on that.

Black brackets the narrative at this point as an element of Jewish and Christian belief, and, moreover, allows that multiple interpretations are possible on discrete points. However, there is no question that the event, as reported, did occur. Clearly, if Isaac was a certain age when his father took him to the wilderness to be slaughtered, then it follows that his father must have taken him to the wilderness to be slaughtered. Hence, the historical reality of this story is established through the metanarrative. The issue of whether this might be a metaphor or what different meanings it could have is simply blocked as its historicity is affirmed. And, perhaps more significantly, if the students do engage in a reinterpretation of the text, it does not occur in the classroom.

In Mr. Black's view, the miracle disclaimer fulfills his basic constitutional responsibilities. And it does provide a token space for interpretive variation, but Black defines the limits for interpretive exercise. While he carves out space for individual conscience, the disclaimer reiterates the historical authority of the Bible and discourages inquiry into the nature of that authority or the validity of its message.

BLACK'S DILEMMA: HISTORY, FAITH, AND THE MORAL ORDER

Morris Black is conscious that he holds beliefs that should not surface in the classroom: "I try to keep it historical," he tells us in an interview, "but however knowing that for me as a believer, I'm good with it as a religious teaching. But as I'm teaching it, that can't be all that comes through." By cleaving to what he takes as strict historical discipline, Black strives to keep in check the personal commitment he has to the Bible as a religious teaching. Yet, for Black, the historian and the believer can be kept only so far apart in practice, because the historical "aspect" of the Bible is infused with a religious and moral message. It may be history, but this history is deeply connected to a moral vision. "When you cover Bible History," Black explains to us, it is almost impossible to separate the rote sequence of events from the "undercurrent of morality all woven through it. It's kind of like a common thread that goes all the way through." It is a history with a message. Thus, while on one axis, teaching Bible as history is clearly distinct, for Black, from devotion, on a different axis, the fabric of biblical history makes it difficult for him to make a clear distinction. History, as a discipline, is the foundation for his notion of educational legitimacy, but at those points where the nature of biblical history seems to erode the firm disciplinary boundary, Mr. Black experiences a stark tension that he finds difficult either to explain or to resolve.

If Bible History is history with a message, what kind of message does it announce? The basic theme of his class is that the "Old Testament" contains a chronicle of the history of a real people—the Israelites. These people had a unique relationship with God, who agreed to protect them if they obeyed God's will. When history records that they do not obey these commandments, God punished them. For Black, this is important both because of the connection of the people of Israel to Jesus and Christianity, and also because of the connection of the Israelites to a God who continues *to this day* to reward and punish individuals and nations. Communicating the connection without infringing on the Constitution is a concern.

Mr. Black tells us that he personally has a clear sense of a "common thread" that runs all the way through the narratives he covers in this Bible History class. That thread is a moral conviction interwoven in all of Israel's experience.

Q: I was just wondering if you could summarize that thread.
A: [Laughs] I don't know.
Q: I mean, I was just thinking, that one of the threads that I get is that when you disobey God, there are consequences.
A: Yeah. Well, to a Christian or to a Jew, that's the whole message of the Old Testament.

The moral dimension to the "Old Testament," for Mr. Black, ultimately turns on obedience: those who adhere to God's commands are rewarded, while those who disobey are punished. This pattern is not simply present within the narratives; it is what a contemporary believer is supposed to derive from the experience of reading.

> To a believing modern-day Christian or a Jew, you look back at the Old Testament and then you read the New Testament and one of the messages is that Israel blew it. And that's the biggest simplification ever, but they had all these laws and they didn't follow them, and they blew it, and here's what happened as a result of that. And, yes, the Assyrians invaded here and destroyed this part of it, and then history records that the Babylonians, they came in here, the Bible tells why. I mean—to a believing modern-day Christian, modern-day Jew, and they're supposed to learn from that.

His final lecture for the course conveys this message through a sweeping survey of three centuries of the history of Israel from the division of the kingdoms after the death of Solomon until the destruction of Jerusalem by Babylon. Black intended the lecture to document the decline and fall of Israel, and it is critical to the purpose of the course; it is where the Bible tells "why" and not simply "what." For Mr. Black, this segment of Israel's history uncovers the logic of biblical narrative, and without it, Bible History becomes an assortment of dates, peoples, and kings.

But here is where Mr. Black experiences a tension. This moral message that he perceives in the biblical history of Israel belongs to its "faith-based aspect." While this "faith-based aspect" is embedded in the history, Mr. Black does not feel that it can be the subject of his instruction, or the sole subject.

There's just a constant sense that I have that this has to be presented as a history course and the conflict there is that the Bible is presented as—I mean, there's a historical aspect, but the historical aspect is tied in directly with a faith-based aspect. And as a Christian looking back on the historical aspect, I can't separate the faith-based from the historical-based. I just can't. I wasn't brought up like that. I can't in my mind do that. But I have to create an outlet in the classroom for the students to be able to separate the faith-based from the historical if they are not a believer. At least I feel like I have to.

Good history, for Black, makes the past available to the present. The dilemma for Black is that the only means he can see to achieve this end in Bible History involves employing the "faith-based" aspect. The necessity to separate the "faith-based" from the "historical" derives, in his understanding, from the requirement to make the public space of the classroom open to all students even "if they are not a believer." Mr. Black is painfully aware of the tension that this constitutional mandate creates for him.

I teach the class and sometimes in my mind I'm thinking that—in my mind, I've got to think that the ACLU is sitting over there in one of the desks, and I feel that it's important to be careful . . . If I cross over into making it potentially faith-based then I run the risk of raising a red flag with somebody, and so that's always in the back of my mind.

At the same time, Mr. Black acknowledges that draining the history of this "faith-based" aspect runs a different risk. It might distort, in his view, the nature of the subject matter.

I suppose you could teach the class and just totally bypass the faith-based, and it would be very factual. It would be a lot of numbers and military victories and, you know, who the kings are, approximately what date did what king serve, and some of the decisions that they made. But, because you're studying about a people that their national identity and their religion was one and the same, it would be a very empty, it would be a very hollow, class.

This is the heart of the tension Mr. Black experiences. The Bible presents to him two faces: a "history-based aspect," which falls into his purview as a history teacher, and a "faith-based aspect," which belongs to him as a believer. In his understanding, he is constitutionally permitted to present the former in the classroom, but the emergence of the latter is fraught with problems and runs "the risk of raising a red flag" with potential critics. However, to be unable to confront the students with this message is to create a "very hollow class" that fails to connect the students with the core message of the Bible, though it might bristle with information. We suspect that many teachers of Bible History experience this dilemma, and it is to Mr. Black's credit that he is able to articulate it so clearly. He experiences the constitutional requirement as an external constraint, which obstructs his means to connect the concrete events of Israel's past to the eternal realm of God's moral order. For Black, however, the ultimate meaning of Israel's past is to be sought precisely in that order. As a consequence, it is necessary for him to enlist the metanarrative tacitly to fill the gap between history and moral order that he does not feel he can directly fill. We revisit this dilemma in the next chapter to consider whether other tools might enable Black to broach this gap. For now, however, let us ask: what is this metanarrative that Black wants the students to recognize?

The metanarrative for Mr. Black is this: the Bible is the true story of a morally fragile people aware for the first time in history of God's plan, and who, like America, often fall short of it. This narrative surfaces at key moments in the class, but only briefly and indirectly. Nevertheless, it provides the class with its significance and gives the students the larger meaning he feels they need.

Mr. Black is aware of one powerful external constraint: his vision of the ACLU lawyer, whom he imagines as ready to pounce upon any missteps in the classroom. Consciousness of this legal authority intervenes at times to inhibit the moral narrative. In such cases, he can rely silently on communal authority without making it a visible part of the class. Instead of employing the class, as in Tearville-Tapscott, to make visible the connection between the school and the community, Mr. Black can rely comfortably on the authority of communal experience to *supplement* the explicit instruction of the class. He tells us that as many as two-thirds of his students "have been brought up on the Bible." This estimation corresponds to our own experience of the class. We visited Ridge High one day when a local Christian youth group was preparing for a weekend retreat. More than half of the students in the class sported T-shirts that proclaimed their membership in the group, creating a sea of powder blue that gave visible testimony to the church's presence within the classroom. Mr. Black might resolve the tension he personally experiences between the "history-based" and "faith-based" aspects of the class by allowing the moral "message" to be inferred by those who already know it.

STEERING AS A PEDAGOGICAL STRATEGY

Not all teachers are as indirect as Mr. Black, and blocking is not the only strategy available to deliver a message of faith. Mr. Black's colleague, Aaron Milsap, feels it is quite legitimate to allow his students to voice directly the moral connection between the history of the Israelites and the fate of modern nations. In our interview, Milsap reviews for us the events that led to the collapse of the divided kingdoms of Israel.

> The students see the rising and falling of nations, and in the Bible History class it is repeated over and over and over again, that every time the Israelites turn their back on God, that they fail, and they fail hard. . . . And so, we see destruction and my Bible History class really, really focuses on that. But what does that mean for our country? They're not wanting us to have prayer in school anymore. The majority of my class will be Christian students and these Christian students will bring this out. A lot. "We're like the Israelite nation," they'll say. This is not me. This is students speaking. "We're like the Israelite nation, Mr. Milsap. We're turning our back." How many countries do you see with a Sin City? How many countries do you see celebrating a Mardi Gras festival and doing the lewd acts that you see there? And they bring this out. This is stuff that I know, but they bring this out!

Mr. Milsap encourages questions from students and provides space for their views to be expressed. For example, where Mr. Black provides space for students to silently make their own private connection between history and faith, relying on the faith convictions of the local evangelical community to fill in the gaps, Mr. Milsap relies on the students themselves to supply that connection for the class. Black communicates a metamessage, hoping that it will be received appropriately; Milsap provides his students with the space to voice their own religious message. Yet given that the topic is the Bible, Milsap tells us that those "who do not know a lot about the Scripture, or about Bible in general, sit back and listen."

They don't debate." In practice, space is provided mostly for religiously Christian students to voice their understanding of the Bible and conscripts the self-identified Christian students to draw the moral inferences that Milsap perceives the Bible to suggest. Milsap is quite active in this matter. He frequently "steers" the class to make the connections that he wants them to make.

By "steering," we mean a mechanism of classroom control included in most teachers' repertoire of techniques. Consider a student who demonstrates difficulty with two-digit multiplication. When asked "how much is 10 times 13," she only manages an embarrassed silence. Okay, the teacher might continue: "how much is "10 times 10?" "100." And "10 times 3?" "That would be thirty." "Very good," the teacher affirms, "and how much is 100 plus 30?""A hundred and thirty?""Excellent!" This hypothetical exchange exemplifies "steering" as a device teachers use to set up the logic that elicits a preferred response.

Steering often is employed where there is a line of reasoning or an answer that a teacher perceives as correct, but where there is potential for students to disrupt the preferred direction or to challenge the "correct answer." Teachers can use steering when they want to encourage participation and engage the students in problem solving while also leading them toward "the right answer." Steering may involve leading questions, limiting the number of legitimate alternatives, or in lieu of verbal cues, calling on reliable students while ignoring others. Other, nonverbal steering cues are tone of voice, eye contact (or avoidance), where the teacher stands and students sit, and how praise is offered or withheld. Whatever the mechanism, the goal of steering is to lead the student to a "correct" answer without discouraging a certain amount of give and take. In Mr. Milsap's class, his religiously Christian students take the lead in explicating the moral lessons to the class. Their greater familiarity with the Bible is allowed to give them a certain advantage and helps to quell less-informed students from voicing opinions.

Steering sets the logic of the students' encounter with the text of the Bible to support an inevitable, even if unstated, conclusion about its historical and moral truth. Blocking involves maintaining and reinforcing a trajectory of belief by closing off alternative readings and opportunities for analysis or critical reflection. Both reinforce the message that the Bible is an accurate report of historical events that provides clear moral guidelines for both individuals and nations. In steering, the message is delivered actively; the teacher sets the logic so that only one conclusion can reasonably be drawn. In blocking, the message is set passively as the only message available. In employing either technique, the teacher is attempting to respect constitutional constraints. Neither Milsap nor Mr. Black *consciously* attempts to evade constitutional neutrality. Quite the opposite: they seek to mirror communal values in the classroom without overstepping First Amendment restrictions—at least as they see them. The difficulty, as exemplified in Black's dilemma, is that the problem is deeper than observing constitutional boundaries; it also entails the conception of the formation of a public. To explore this aspect of the limits of a Bible History course, we return to an issue we raised earlier: the requirement for schools to provide recognition to their local constituencies without totalizing that worldview by nonrecognition or misrecognition of alternatives.

Chapter 4

MISRECOGNITION AND NONRECOGNITION
A Caution for Religion Courses

Staying on the surface in Tearville-Tapscott and Ridge reinforces a default moral message that God rewards virtue and punishes sin and also provides recognition to the values and beliefs of the dominant Christian community. In turn, the schools gain credibility with the religiously Christian segments of the community. Recognition of the community's values, consequently, is a valuable—perhaps even essential—function of the school. In their different ways, Ridge and Tearville-Tapscott both employ their Bible courses, in part, to provide public recognition to the community. A significant challenge for these districts, then, is to provide the desired recognition to the visibly dominant Christian community while affording equal recognition to other elements of their constituency. Problems arise for public education when the recognition of one group comes at the cost of the *misrecognition* or *nonrecognition* of another. Misrecognition is the assignment of people to a different and stigmatized group. Nonrecognition occurs when others are viewed as instruments for our own ends and are denied recognition on their own terms. Charles Taylor explains what is at stake for democracies when equal recognition is denied.

> Equal recognition is not just the appropriate model for a healthy democratic society. Its refusal can inflict damage on those who are denied it. . . . The projection of an inferior or demeaning image on another can actually distort and oppress, to the extent that the image is internalized.[1]

Misrecognition is frequently the byproduct of totalizing a single religious tradi-tion, that is, by treating one's own faith tradition as the apex of human experi-ence or as the sum of all other experiences. Totalizing occurs when one tradition is taught as the only acceptable tradition and other traditions are dismissed as inferior or interpreted only through its light. Within a private religious school this is allowed, perhaps even expected in some contexts. Such misrecognition, however, can have serious consequences when permitted in public-school set-tings, particularly if it supports the devaluing of minority members of the com-munity.

MISRECOGNITION: THE ATHEIST IN THE CLASSROOM

A common example of misrecognition occurs when a person is assigned an in-ferior or stigmatized status because of some irrelevant attribute, such as skin color or gender. However, another kind of misrecognition occurs when a per-son's belief is stigmatized or marked as inferior, or when pressure is exerted to accept an alien belief, or when a person is manipulated in order to change his or her core belief.

Aaron Milsap recalls to us a particular student, whom he affectionately re-fers to as "our atheist." This student told him after one class that she had been diagnosed with a brain tumor. "Two days later," Milsap recollects, "we're talking about the people who had taken the ark and God had placed tumors." This story, which spans from 1 Samuel 5.1 to 1 Samuel 7.2, concerns the misfortunes that fell upon the Philistines after they captured the Ark of the Covenant from Israel and brought it to their own city. In this account, God countered this sei-zure by inflicting the Philistines with a disease, variously translated as boils or tumors. (Milsap chooses to read it as "tumors.") The Philistines suffered this plague until they returned the ark to Israel, which they did after a great deal of consideration.

This story is not usually part of the Ridge County syllabus, but in this case Milsap veered from the curriculum for a specific purpose. The reason he told that story was so that "they would see what would happen if you went and did something immoral, or against God's will or God's wishes. And I think that the Old Testament brings a lot of that out." He then reported that one student asked: "Does God still punish today?" As Mr. Milsap recalls, his student with the tumor laughed: "She said, 'I guess I had better start believing.'" In that instant, the work of the class shifted from a presentation of an ancient narrative, which might have implications for modern circumstances, to consideration of the existential condition of the students. Milsap's atheist student later visited him after class. He recalled that meeting in the following way.

> You see I had some explaining to do to that young lady. I had some one-on-one conversation with her later. Because she's like, "Do you think God's punishing me?" I say, "Well, first of all, do you believe in God? I mean what would be the difference? Because if you're an atheist, you don't believe that there is a God to punish you."

The student extends the classroom session as she interprets her own crisis through the lens of the Philistines. The logic is simple, albeit flawed: the fact that the Philistines sinned and came down with tumors does not, of course, mean that anyone with a tumor is a sinner. The logic steers students to the intended conclusion without requiring the instructor to make it explicit: the consequences of sin are visible, repent before it is too late! Instead of opening up the logic and allowing the student some other interpretation, he simply reminds her, albeit implicitly, of the sin of nonbelief: what would be the difference because if you're an atheist you don't believe that there is a God who punishes you?

It would likely take a team of lawyers to determine whether there are constitutional issues in this instance.[2] Nonetheless, the educational transaction is a clear example of misrecognition, where the instructor uses the lesson to implicitly stigmatize her (non) belief and then steer students toward belief. He does this by setting the premises through assigned readings, translating terms one way (tumors) rather than another (boils), responding to expected questions, blocking reasonable alternative conclusions, closing down certain interpretations, and using the brain tumor as a "teachable moment" to prompt a crisis of (non) faith in the student.

Our interest, however, in Mr. Milsap's handling of the situation goes beyond these manifest grounds for criticism. He told us this story because it represented to him an example of *successful* teaching. He displayed particular pride in three points: (1) that a student raised the question of whether God still punishes now; (2) that he responded to this question solely with biblical sources;

and (3) that this classroom exchange enabled him to work more individually with the student herself, who later, when he asked, gave him permission to pray for her health.[3] All three of these points capture something for which advocates often yearn: the capacity of Bible classes to lead to transformation of the students. Milsap sets the stage though manipulating the information the students receive by changing the syllabus, and thus encouraging the atheist to connect the biblical past to her present. For Mr. Milsap, his stage setting works as the student begins to question her nonbelief.

After our work with Ridge High, we presented this incident to a group of teachers from other school districts. The teachers uniformly judged this to be highly unprofessional teaching. In their view, Mr. Milsap should not have taught this lesson given the student's condition and the story of the Philistines and the tumors should have been omitted from the classroom—this adjustment would be an accommodation for the student's potential sensitivity to the situation. In their view, it was the duty of the teacher to avoid creating a situation where the student would identify her own present circumstances with the figures of an ancient narrative. The difference between Milsap and the teachers' group is in part one of professional ethic. Where Milsap sees the opportunity to steer a student to a pathway of salvation, the teachers' group fears the potential compromise of the student's autonomy. They worry that she is being consigned to a role in an ongoing historical narrative where she and the Philistines experience the wrath of God for their transgressions.

When Mr. Milsap taught that God punished the Philistines by inflicting them with tumors he might well have been teaching a lesson that other teachers had taught before without incident. The lesson takes on a different meaning when there is a student in class who has a tumor and when that student is especially vulnerable because she does not share the beliefs of the teacher or her classmates. Mr. Milsap likely intended no disrespect and was truly concerned about his student's health. We take his offer to pray for her as a mark of genuine concern and if *it* raises legal issues because it happened in a public space, it would raise them whether the student were an atheist or a devout Christian. It is rather his failure to make an appropriate adjustment that makes this episode educationally problematic. He failed to respect the student's beliefs and took advantage of her condition to try to manipulate them. In doing so, he attempted to consume her identity within his own and failed to provide her with the recognition she was due. He failed to adjust his lesson in a way that would protect her dignity. (Indeed, since this episode was not on the syllabus he actually seemed to go out of his way to include it.)

The issue is not only constitutional. He taught his lesson; she came to his office; he offered his sympathy and asked if he could include her in his regular daily prayers. We strongly suspect that Mr. Milsap meets the expectations of most people in this religiously conservative community. He is an energetic, enthusiastic, caring person, and most of his students and their parents likely value his teaching. Yet if the issue is not constitutional (and we are not qualified to make the legal judgment), it is certainly educational. The problem is a professional, even if it were not a legal or communal, one. He offers an expression of concern that in other situations would have been appropriate. Here it is not. The episode fails to meet appropriate educational standards, and fails an important test of educational legitimacy. A student is misrecognized and hence disrespected for her (non) belief.

While blocking and steering are reasonable pedagogical strategies in many situations, both pedagogies are problematic when teaching Bible History in the context of public education. They assume that there is a correct answer and thus close off questions about the authority of the Bible as a historical text. In this way, they inhibit the possibility of richly textured discussion of the various ways the Bible can be read by different communities. The result is to give recognition to only the more literal-inclined religious communities. Recognition is provided to a restricted group and others are left out of the discussion.

RETURN TO BLACK'S DILEMMA: A POSSIBLE SOLUTION

It would be understandable if skeptics concluded from these accounts that Bible courses should not be taught in public schools. We think, however, that there is an alternative lesson that can be drawn. We noted earlier the gap between the conception of "history" in biblical scholarship and that which shapes the classroom endeavors at Ridge. Biblical scholars apply the tools of historical criticism in an attempt to define the understandings, ideologies, and perceptions of the original producers and receivers of the text. Black and Milsap understand the discipline of Bible History as the use of the text to describe events as they actually occurred. For the biblical scholar, historical investigation aims to facilitate an encounter—to the extent possible—with the consciousness of an author, while for Black the historical author is a window through which the historian discerns the event. One difficulty Black himself recognized as arising from this conception of his discipline is that it created a tension between his need of a faith-based dimension to make the history meaningful to the class and the constitutional constraints he perceived on his role as a teacher. There are a number of reasons that teachers, such as Black, who identify as conservative Christians might resist the use of conventions of historical critical scholarship, either in personal study or in classroom use. These range from doctrinal convictions about the divine origin of the Bible to pedagogical anxiety for the potential impact on students. Yet biblical scholarship could be used to advantage in teaching Bible History courses.

Let us consider as an example the narrative that is at the moral center of how both Milsap and Black teach their Bible History courses: the rise and collapse of the monarchy of Israel. Biblical scholars typically regard this long narrative, which spans six books of the Bible, as a part of a monumental history, known as the Deuteronomistic History (DH). This history reached its final form after the collapse of the monarchy in the Babylonian conquest of the sixth century BCE.[4] Scholars have concluded that this long narrative probably was edited several times before reaching the form in which we have it today. The editors undertook this task in light of the agony of Israel's exile by the conquering Babylonians and attempted to understand and explain how this catastrophe could occur.[5] The DH, consequently, relates a narrative from a particular point of view and in order to comprehend a particular situation—much like any historian writing in any time. For the anonymous editor of DH, the blame for Israel's collapse rested squarely on its failure to observe the requirements of the nation's covenant with its God, and the history is both an attempt to face up to this acute sense of failure and a call to the nation to renew its covenantal loyalty.[6] This is similar to the moral worldview that both Black and Milsap want their students to adopt, with the qualification that the editor of DH did not see—as Black suggests—that Israel's failure was irredeemable. The history indeed exposes what the historian regards as Israel's deep failings but also envisions the possibility for the people's renewal; for DH, the monarchy's collapse is not the same as the end of Israel.

It is thus important to note that Black and Milsap's reading of Israel's history is congruous to some extent with the moral judgment entailed in the Deuteronomistic History as understood by its scholarly reconstruction. It is equally important to note, however, an important difference between the scholarly re-construction of DH and their Bible History course. For the biblical scholar, the DH reveals how a school of authors and editors living in specific conditions made sense of the vicissitudes of Israel's history, what pattern they imposed upon the flux of events. To read 1 and 2 Kings this way is to attempt to enter the horizons of a specific person under specific historical circumstances and to acknowledge that other explanations for the monarchy's collapse and alter-nate prescriptions for Israel's renewal could have been—and indeed were—advanced by other members of the exilic community.[7] By contrast, insofar as Black and Milsap present the biblical books as transparent windows to events as they occurred, they treat the events narrated as self-interpreting independent of the writers that report them. This mode of presentation shifts the work of the class from interpreting one response to disaster—that of the Deuterono-mistic Historian—toward discerning the eternal pattern of God's judgment. The effect is simultaneously de-historicizing (as the mode of inquiry does not incorporate how the reports were constructed) and totalizing (as it presents the destruction of Israel as an example of God's timeless will). The totalizing nature of the reading emerges in Mr. Black's summation to us of the moral of the tragic history of 1 and 2 Kings. We quoted it in the previous chapter, but it bears repeating here.

> To a believing modern-day Christian or a Jew, you look back at the Old Testa-ment and then you read the New Testament and one of the messages is that Israel blew it. And that's the biggest simplification ever, but they had all these laws and they didn't follow them, and they blew it, and here's what happened as a result of that. And, yes, the Assyrians invaded here and destroyed this part of it, and then history records that the Babylonians, they came in here, the Bible tells why. I mean—to a believing modern-day Christian, modern-day Jew, and they're supposed to learn from that.

There is only one message that Mr. Black can identify from the history, and it is one that is accessible only to believing modern-day Christians and Jews. As this is a message directed toward believers, Black locates it in the "faith-based aspect" he identifies in the Bible, which he struggles to keep from entering openly into the classroom. Nonetheless, the conservative communal subtext is unchecked as the only means to appropriate this history. Past is prologue and Milsap's students draw the conclusions that the sins of pornography, homosexuality, abortion, and greed bring nations to their knees. We would not be prepared to see any of this as crossing any constitutional lines. At the same time, as discussed in the beginning of the chapter, the move toward a totalizing message threatens the principle of equal recognition that is vital to the construction and maintenance of civic democracy. Equal recognition in this case would be advanced by an approach to the long recital of Israel's history that emphasized the character of its narration as the key to approaching that history. Ideally, a teacher would place the DH into dialogue with other responses to the tragedy of exile, such as the books of Jeremiah and Ezekiel, and the sections of the book of Isaiah (chs. 40–55) generally held to relate to the exilic situation.

It would be incumbent upon a teacher who approached the material this way to acknowledge to the class that the DH is a scholarly construct—failure to do so would risk another form of totalization. It is not our proposal that a Bible History class addressing this period of Israelite history must use this framework. What the example of the Deuteronomistic History illustrates for us is that Mr. Black's dilemma is not simply the result of a teacher's difficulty in checking his faith commitments at the schoolhouse door. The difficulty confronting the Bible History course runs more deeply. Black's dilemma reflects his view that the meaning of the Bible rests in an appropriation of its unchanging and eternal moral order. Israel's history is taught as significant for its exemplifying character; it is not a series of contingent events, but an instantiation of God's will and how God ensures that will becomes operative in society.

In contrast, a teacher who took seriously the task of empowering students by teaching them to mediate a familiar narrative could still accommodate the moral worldview of DH as one of the various responses Israel collectively made to the experience of exile. That message then could be available for discussion as it belongs quite particularly to the worldview of an individual author (or editor) and other responses could be considered. In this approach, the theme of judgment on Israel would be historically mediated, and perhaps also balanced, as some scholars have done, with themes of divine grace also identified within DH.[8] But this would require that students be taught that the narrative was constructed in response to specific historical conditions, serving to construct a specific collective Israelite identity. Such an approach could resolve the dichotomy that Mr. Black perceives between the historical and faith dimensions of the text.

We concede that the skeptic does have a point: this resolution would come with a price, one that may exceed what the Ridge High School community can easily accept. To teach the historical books of the Hebrew Bible in this fashion would be to convey to students a history with a "message," but—and this is significant—that message would belong to the ancient author and to the readers of his own time—not necessarily to readers of all times. Moreover, this then opens the possibility that the record of events in the history is not a transparent window to the events themselves. The concept of DH implies that the aims and intentions of a human author filter the reported events. That is, the Bible would not provide students with direct access to the events in and of themselves, but to the *narration* of those events, and the class would then need to wrestle with the presuppositions and biases of the *narrator*. While this approach would preserve the perception that Mr. Black expresses that the historical narrative of the Israelite kingship is a moral history, it would *interrupt* a deterministic application of that history to the contemporary world, either individually or socially, allowing the students to open up questions that Black and Milsap feel are better left closed. Yet it is hard to escape the conclusion that these are less than conscious choices on the parts of Black and Milsap. For both teachers, narrative and belief are intertwined, never to be consciously detached, serving as the unconscious engines of their presentation of Bible History. For other teachers, however, bringing *alternative* approaches out into the open might be a first step in addressing the skeptic's rejection.

As for us, we wonder whether Bible History courses can successfully avoid the tendency to totalization and open themselves to alternative appropriations of the text, especially when the purpose of the course is understood as the identification of the events rather than an exploration of the narratives. In the next chapter, we consider an approach that shifts from the history the Bible tells to the history of the Bible itself. We will take up the possibilities this offers in providing equal recognition to multiple communities and diverse readers of the Bible.

Chapter 5

THE BIBLE AND ITS INFLUENCE
Instilling Equal Recognition into the Curriculum

While the Bible History programs we examined in the first chapters served the dominant local religious community, they failed to provide adequate recognition to other voices. The result was the totalization of a narrow Christian perspective and the submergence of all other points of view to this perspective. This did not seem to us to be a conscious lapse. Rather the teachers taught what they knew, seemingly uninformed about the views of other traditions and ignorant about their own ignorance. However, Bible History courses are not representative of all Bible courses, and in this chapter we look at a program that makes a conscious effort not just to follow the Constitution and avoid the wrath of the ACLU, but to provide a reasonably inclusive program, one that takes into account a variety of different standpoints. The course we looked at is called the Bible and Its Influence, a one semester or yearlong elective taught mostly to high school juniors and seniors.

Courses that center on the influence of the Bible are a growing alternative to Bible History. These courses focus on the various uses of the Bible instead of attempting either to recover the original meaning of the biblical text or to reconstruct the events toward which that text might point. Because they bracket the question of the truth of the Bible they can avoid many of the constitutional concerns that can arise when the Bible is presented as a historical text. The growth of these courses can be attributed in no small part to the influence of the Bible Literacy Project (BLP), which is committed to promoting "academic courses" about the Bible in schools across the country.

Our interest in this approach to classroom study of the Bible stems, in part, from the potential it affords to incorporate the goal of equal recognition into the curriculum. In this way, the Bible and Its Influence may facilitate the fulfillment of the "welcoming function" of the public school, as discussed in chapter 2. We turn in this chapter to Jordan Country High School as an example of a community that has adopted this course, including the textbook, *The Bible and Its Influence*, developed by the BLP.

Jordan County is in some respects similar to Ridge and Tapscott counties. It is a rural school district, reliant on poultry farming and long-distance trucking for its economic well-being. Demographically, the county is very homogenous—about 97 percent Caucasian and culturally Protestant. There are no synagogues or mosques within the school district and there is just one Catholic church. It is, however, substantially more prosperous than either of the two other counties explored. Both family income and house values are close to the national median. In measures of educational achievement, Jordan County also scores at or near state and national averages.[1]

Sam Watson is a social-studies teacher with seventeen years of experience at the time of this study, and his primary teaching assignment is American government. He graduated from Jordan County High School and holds a bachelor's degree in political science. He taught for a number of years in the district's middle school before moving on to the high school. In addition to the Bible course, he also teaches an Advanced Placement course in American history and a course in American government. Watson believes that his background in American government and constitutional law is one reason that the school principal approached him to be the instructor for the newly proposed Bible class. He also speculates that his public involvement with Christian groups at the high school had identified him as possessing necessary familiarity with the subject matter. Watson is quick to add, "Not because he wanted a Christian to teach it from a Christian perspective, but that he expected, I think, that my background knowledge of the Bible would lend itself well to creating a course like this." Watson, however, has some doubts and sees his reputation as a churchgoing Christian as a mixed blessing, because it places certain expectations on him that he feels may be inconsistent with his role as a public-school teacher.

THE DEVELOPMENT OF THE JORDAN COUNTY COURSE

In contrast to Ridge and Tapscott counties, the impetus for the introduction of the course in Jordan County began with the school board, rather than citizens or community interest groups. As the administrators of the school district related the story to us, the drive to develop the course began with an explicit desire to extend an element of character education in the district's curriculum. Dr. Daniel Ballard, superintendent of Jordan County schools, came to the district in the wake of a massive fraud that left the district with a substantial deficit. To help restore community trust he prompted the school board to develop a vision that would direct a renewed sense of the school district's mission and heal the community together. The board responded by reaffirming, in Ballard's words, the community's "very biblical" focus, centering its vision on the "core values" of the Bible and the "time-honored traditions," signaled by the motto "in God we trust." From this process, Ballard continues, the board president approached him to inquire how these core values might be implemented in an individual course. It was his view, moreover, that while the district had adequate character education units in place in the elementary- and middle-school levels, a vacuum existed in this area in the high school. In Ballard's view, the Bible course was directly linked from its outset to character education, which Ballard understands in terms of moral formation, and as aiding the student's "character development."

The board and superintendent both identified the development of a Bible class as a component to wider curricular and communal goals focused on the cultivation of sound character. Legal and constitutional issues were then left for Ballard and his staff to work out. As the idea moved outside the board to the superintendent and then to the principal and the teacher, it became increasingly refined, and Douglas Wells, principal of Jordan High, reminded the board on a repeated basis that such a class would necessarily be an "academic course." The challenge facing Wells and the instructor of the course, Watson, was to translate these goals of moral formation into a course that did not promote one particular vision of morality or equated genuine morality with a religious worldview.

The board left the determination of the actual structure and content of the course in the hands of the school administration and its faculty. The school could have followed the path of Ridge and Tapscott in developing a Bible History course. Ballard, however, was acutely aware of the legal challenges to which schools could be subject, and a recent court decision against another school district in a case concerning a course that promoted the concept of intelligent design as an alternative to evolution provided a cautionary tale. "I wasn't going to follow that path," he told us. "I really wasn't going to do it. I didn't think they [i.e., the school board that authorized the instruction on intelligent design] did enough research in my opinion of what they needed to do." Ballard believed his goal could be achieved by adding a high-school Bible course to the character-education program, which the district already had in place in the elementary and middle schools. He felt that the goal of improving character provided the course with a legitimate secular purpose (in keeping with the Lemon test) and hence would meet court scrutiny, if required to do so. Thus, in his view, the course simply complemented work that had begun in the earlier grades, and that had never been challenged as unconstitutional.

As Ballard explains it, Americans have a strong sense of good and bad, and in the vocabulary they use to label those values "there tends to be a trail back to religion and Bible." Consequently, to know what prominent American leaders meant in their rhetoric—Martin Luther King Jr., for example—it is essential to know how that rhetoric is formed by that trail. While Ballard allows that good people do not have to be religious, the proposed course as he described it certainly would have advanced the perception that a belief in the Bible is an essential part of a good character. It is notable for our purposes that Ballard's conception of character education is tied less to codes of obedience than to a search for moral exemplars. In this way, his vision for the course already moves away from the discernment of a permanent moral code to the usage and reception of a tradition. In Ballard's view, this shift from biblical *text* to biblical *influence* was both in keeping with constitutional guidelines and consistent with the board's aims of promoting character education in the district's lone high school. In characterizing the intention of the course, Ballard displays a firm sense of the distinction between "teaching religion" and "teaching about religion" developed by the national education societies and canonized by the Supreme Court in *Abington* and subsequent case law.

We in no way, shape, or form contend that we are teaching the Bible. We aren't teaching religion and we aren't teaching the Bible. However, the influences of very influential people in our country, the making of our country, the continual development of our country, is being done by people who are influenced by the Bible or are influenced by religion or are influenced by their faith and belief. We are *not* teaching the Bible, and we are *not* teaching religion. We are creating an awareness of how those things impact [influential people].

The textbook selection was the single most important decision, in Ballard's view, in shaping the course's aims and the identity of the class. As Ballard described the process, he told the board: "You know, we create a curriculum and then select a textbook. We have to do it the opposite way this time. We have to really focus on an approved textbook that might get the controversial people on board." We do not know whom he had in mind when referring to the "controversial people." He may be referring to potential objectors to a Bible curriculum in the public school. If so, then the competition for equal recognition also made its influence felt at a formative stage in the development of the course. The selection of the textbook fell to the instructor of the course, Sam Watson, who consulted instructors of courses in other districts and reviewed two potential curricula: *The Bible in History and Literature*, produced by the NCBCPS, and *The Bible and Its Influence*, by the Bible Literacy Project. As mentioned at the outset of this study, these are two most widespread national curricula, marketed throughout the United States. Even though they squabble between themselves, together, these two movements have made it easier for public schools like Jordan County High to develop Bible courses. Before investigating Jordan's specific experience, it is an opportune time to discuss in more detail the character of these two curricula.

A BRIEF DETOUR: EMERGENCE OF NATIONALLY MARKETED CURRICULA

Academic instruction in the Bible, as opposed to the use of Bible readings in devotional exercises that opened the school day, began to take root in the opening decades of the twentieth century. Without any firm conventions or available materials, numerous school districts began to experiment with developing their own frameworks for such instruction, employing a wide range of formats. Most of these experiments were local in nature and embodied the aims and purposes of individual instructors or the religious associations that supported and oversaw the curriculum development. Attempts to develop wider networks of shared pedagogical experience and subject-matter knowledge were few and far between, and typically failed to attract widespread implementation. Bible courses continue to be locally developed and implemented—often from an assemblage of materials available at hand or via Internet resources. In the last two decades, however, there have also emerged the two organizations mentioned earlier that offer comprehensive curricular packages on the Bible. These organizations have assembled teams of publicists and lobbyists, seeking to shape legislative initiatives that would increase the market for their products.

The earlier of the two curricula, the National Council's *Bible in History and Literature* (BHL), provides an outline for a yearlong Bible course divided between (in the curriculum's titles) "Old Testament" and "New Testament." The curriculum suggests the King James Version of the Bible as its primary "textbook," although it does not require any specific translation. The curriculum supports this textbook with a teacher's guide that provides background information, historical and religious contextualization, and makes brief suggestions for lesson plans. This effort began in 1993 in the National Council's home state of North Carolina and subsequently has expanded to almost half of the nation's states, although it is most prominent in rural districts of the American South. At the time of our writing, the organization's website claimed that "our curriculum has been voted into 687 school districts (2,262 high schools) in 38 states."[2] If accurate, these numbers would suggest a remarkable saturation of the potential market by the NCBCPS. This claim, however, had not been independently verified at the time of this writing, in part because NCBCPS has not agreed to release data concerning the use of its curriculum, and some school systems have not cooperated in efforts to determine if the curriculum is used in their districts.[3]

The National Council is an explicitly evangelical Christian organization with strong ties to the religiously and politically conservative family of movements sometimes called "Christian Reconstructionism," which holds that America is, and should be, a "Christian nation."[4] The board of directors is stocked with prominent leaders of conservative Christian circles, including Chuck Norris, the TV martial-arts star turned Christian columnist, and David Barton, the founder and president of the historical advocacy organization, WallBuilders.[5] WallBuilders, which endorses an establishment of the United States as a Christian nation, identifies its educational mission as a restoration of traditional historical instruction that celebrated America's laws as "rooted in Biblical principles."[6] For a number of years, the National Council was a featured participant in the Coral Ridge Ministries "Reclaiming America for Christ" conference, an annual workshop in Florida for training grassroots activists devoted to conservative causes. D. James Kennedy, who was the senior pastor at Coral

Ridge until his death in 2007, produced a promotional video on behalf of the National Council, identifying it as one of the "few bright spots" in the "moral and spiritual darkness in today's public schools."[7]

Evangelical sponsorship and motivation does not itself demonstrate that the curriculum represents a kind of Trojan horse to insinuate Christian doctrine into the public-school classroom. Indeed, the BHL insists that participating teachers avoid devotional usage of biblical texts.[8] Nonetheless, the curriculum has been subject to legal challenge. In 1997, the introduction of the BHL into a Florida school district was challenged by plaintiffs represented by the ACLU and People for the American Way. The plaintiffs argued that the curriculum failed all three prongs of the Lemon test, and the presiding judge applied these criteria in adjudicating a motion for preliminary injunction to prevent the teaching of the two courses, Bible History I and II, in Lee County schools. The federal court issued in part the requested preliminary injunction, *Gibson v. Lee County School Board*, partially upholding the plaintiffs' petition, declaring that the New Testament portion of the curriculum could not be taught and that the "Old Testament" curriculum could be taught only with strict monitoring.[9] The school board then settled the case by withdrawing its curriculum in favor of an alternative. More recently, a constitutional challenge to a National Council–based course in Odessa, Texas, was settled when the school district agreed to remove the curriculum from use.[10] Although the NCBCPS claims that 93 percent of school boards "approached" with the curriculum approve its use, there have been in recent years a number of boards that have declined its use, citing concerns about constitutionality.[11]

The second nationally marketed curriculum is published by the Bible Literacy Project (BLP), and consists of a textbook, *The Bible and Its Influence* (BI), the teacher's edition to this book, and a web-based training program, which also offers continuing support to participating teachers.[12] The BLP can trace its roots back, in part, to concerns stimulated by the National Council. The *Gibson* case gave impetus to a broad coalition, which had been taking shape even before the lawsuit, to develop a Bible curriculum securely grounded on Supreme Court precedent. This undertaking pooled the resources of the First Amendment Center, the National Education Association, People for the American Way, and a number of mainstream Jewish, Christian, and Muslim organizations. One key member of this coalition was Chuck Stetson, who at the time was vice president of the National Bible Association, which is best known for its sponsorship of

National Bible Week every year since 1941. Stetson subsequently launched the BLP as an independent venture, with its primary mission being the creation of a Bible course that embodied constitutional guidelines.

The BLP tested an initial version of *The Bible and Its Influence* in a pilot run in several sites, including Memphis, Tennessee, in fall 2002.[13] A second round of testing took place in several pilot school sites in the Pacific Northwest before the official launch of the text in fall of 2005. The BLP cause was assisted by the endorsement it received from high-profile advocates. Charles Haynes, director of the First Amendment Center and an early partner with Stetson, basked in the glow of the text's warm reception: "New high school textbooks don't ordinarily make headlines," Haynes observed. "But," he continued, "*The Bible and Its Influence* is no ordinary textbook." The BLP embodied principles that would promote a "civic school" in which the "democratic first principles" of robust and respectful debate would advance mutual understanding across religious communities. Such a course would not only comply with the First Amendment—it would offer a glimpse of what "schools might look like if we actually lived up to the promise of religious liberty."[14]

The new textbook also secured votes of confidence from significant sectors of the political conservative and evangelical movements. Rich Lowry, editor of the conservative political organ *National Review*, opined, "Rarely is a textbook an occasion for celebration or anything but moaning on the part of students." Lowry made what he called an "emphatic exception" for the "substantial, gorgeously produced, thoroughly vetted volume" of *The Bible and Its Influence*.[15] Endorsements continued to accrue from the National Association of Evangelicals, Chuck Colson, and Alabama political activist Randy Brinson, and warm, if qualified, support from the Baptist Joint Committee for Religious Liberty and the evangelical magazine *Christianity Today*.

Some evangelical opinion makers have cast their lot with the BLP. It has also attracted the fierce opposition of loyalists to the NCBCPS, drawn mainly from the radical Christian right. The NCBCPS proudly brandishes a letter from John Hagee, pastor of Cornerstone Church in San Antonio and director of a small media empire, which characterizes *The Bible and Its Influence* as a "masterful work of deception, distortion and outright falsehoods." He warns that use of the text would further alienate parents from a "public school system undermining the authority and will of the parents."[16]

The dispute between the two curricula divides the evangelical community.

In general, despite some qualms, civil-liberties organizations and some representative religious groups have accepted the BLP as a less problematic, albeit imperfect, alternative to the National Council. The American Jewish Congress and Anti-Defamation League, for example, both endorsed the BLP. When asked by the Jewish publication the *Forward* about this endorsement, officials from both organizations said that they preferred comparative religion courses to classes focused solely on the Bible. Despite these misgivings, they felt compelled to offer an alternative to the National Council curriculum, which they regarded as unacceptable.[17]

Setting aside the factional support that each curriculum garnered, let us now turn to the educational question. How would Watson's course look under each of the two curricula? What difference would it make to both the aims of the course and the way the class would operate?

THE BIBLE IN HISTORY AND LITERATURE AS A CURRICULUM

The BHL divides the course into eighteen units, which are crafted to walk the student through a history of Israel and the early Christian community, and the course conforms, despite a few deviations, to a "Bible History" structure. The units from Genesis to Ruth (units 2–8) all eschew consideration of formal, literary, and rhetorical elements in favor of establishing chronologies. The curriculum is content to establish as the objective for Genesis 1, for example, a linear itemization of the works of each of the seven days, without undertaking any analysis of pattern or motif in shaping the account (e.g., 62f.). This bare chronological approach continues to inform the treatment of the succeeding units, where timelines and charts of events dominate. These are a few of the suggested classroom activities: "Begin a Biblical wall timeline which will continue through the Genesis study" (64); "categorize the major events of the life of the Biblical figure, Joseph" (73); "outline the major events of Moses' birth, childhood, and life in Midian, as presented in the Bible" (81); "identify the twelve tribes of Israel, showing the number of men in each tribe, the governmental structure of the tribes, and the arrangement of the tribes when they camped and traveled" (107). All of these activities presuppose a transparent relationship between the narrative and the events narrated; the primary task assigned to the class is to translate these narratives into linear and tabular data. The inclusion of a separate unit on "literature highlights" (unit 9) emphasizes the dominance of historical categories, by restricting the category of "literature" to a few texts that bear obvious literary markings (e.g., Psalms, Job, Song of Songs).[18] In this way, it reinforces the viewpoint that some biblical books were produced for the purpose of conveying history *apart* from literary considerations, while others were produced for the purpose of literary art *apart* from engagement with their historical context.

The structure of the course, by and large, is set by the framework of historical investigation, punctuated by isolated considerations of literature. One persistent exception, however, disrupts this historical scheme. The teacher is instructed to integrate study of the Psalms and Proverbs in each class "along with the regular, chronologically placed material of the Old Testament/Hebrew Bible" (62). The curriculum intends to interrupt the flow of regular material "as little as possible" (62), but it is expected that by the end of the first semester "fifteen chapters of Proverbs should have been covered" (108). This is a noticeable variance from a historical study for two reasons. First, the Proverbs are a collection of morally didactic sayings strongly oriented toward obedience of authority: the "fear of the Lord is the beginning of knowledge" and the child is instructed to "hear your father's instruction, and do not reject your mother's teaching" (Proverbs 1:7–8). The regular infusion of such bits of instruction becomes a programmatic element parallel to the historical inquiry. The second reason this is of interest is that it preserves at least one of the trappings of the pre-*Abington* devotional use of the Bible, in which readings and recitations of the Psalms and Proverbs figured prominently in mandated school exercises. In this facet of its curriculum, the BHL echoes the traditional moral justifications for Bible reading in a manner that sets this component apart from the historical course of study.

It is of considerable significance that the National Council claims that one of the chief virtues of the BHL is that it employs the Bible itself as the primary textbook. This claim is made operational in the classroom in that the most frequently prescribed classroom activity is to read aloud that day's portion of biblical text. The rationale offered for this approach is that use of the Bible by itself, without the "subjective commentary" of a textbook is more neutral and constitutionally sound than the rival curriculum. For instance, four members of the Texas State Board of Education advocated for the National Council in a letter to the state's school administrators and school boards on precisely these grounds, insinuating that the BLP would be liable to constitutional challenge.

> When selecting a Bible curriculum, it would appear to be a much safer and ultimately accurate approach, to select a curriculum that simply utilizes biblical text rather than subjective commentary and opinion. It follows that subjective commentary and opinion could more easily expose a curriculum to failure to meet constitutional muster, should such ever be questioned.[19]

To hold that the Bible is a textbook rather than an original source appeals to the authority that schools, teachers, and students invest in textbooks as packages of undisputable facts. Not all books or material that find their way into a classroom are textbooks. Literature classes, for instance, often employ a "reader" of selections that are the basis for the classroom work. Bringing a copy of, say, *A Tale of Two Cities*, into the classroom does not make the Dickens classic the textbook of a tenth-grade English class. The authority appeal of a textbook is that it presents an official version of knowledge approved by the requisite authorities (state or district board). The student studies the textbook in order to extract that knowledge, while a student reads from a reader to *experience the text* firsthand.

In history courses, it is customary to distinguish between a history textbook that synthesizes numerous sources to provide an overall perspective and the primary sources that underlie that synthesis. The distinction can be overdrawn: secondary texts can be used as primary sources, and they certainly are not neutral presentations of a value-free body of knowledge. Nonetheless, as the bitter disputes over textbook approval make clear, they are vested with authority as representing a consensus view of a subject. The framework for history and social sciences in California draws a useful distinction. While textbooks enable students to "study" history, the value of the primary source is that it allows student to "investigate" it. To do so, students must learn to subject primary sources to criticism to assess their value for historical inquiry.

> For whom was it written or produced and why? Did the author create it as propaganda for a particular cause? Was it written by an eyewitness? Has the document been translated, and has the format been changed in translation (from poetry into prose, for example)? Most primary sources reflect their author's par-

ticular point of view; this does not make them less valuable. The reader simply needs to be aware of the author's perspective and to avoid taking the source at face value.[20]

This directive for proper use of primary sources correlates neatly with our understanding of the skills and dispositions to be cultivated in humanities classes. It is taken for granted that primary sources are not to be taken at face value as transparent windows to historical events. By designating the Bible as a textbook rather than the source for its course, the National Council obscures an important point about studying the Bible. The Bible is not simply a textbook reporting historical events; it is a historical source that itself requires an investigation. Primary sources demand of the learner a process of inquiry, even before the object of that inquiry can be brought under investigation. A textbook, moreover, is designed for a pedagogical end, and the student is the target reader of a textbook. By contrast, a primary source carries the opposite presumption. In working with a primary source, the investigator presumes that he or she is not the intended audience and that to understand the source is to enter into its horizons by seeking to identify the context in which it was shaped, the function it had for a now distant readership, and the rhetorical means by which it attempted to meet that function.

In framing the Bible as its textbook, the National Council already distances the enterprise from the model of humanities education. We find very little in the body of the BHL curriculum itself that relieves the concern raised by the framing as "textbook." In particular, we find little in the curriculum that would enable students to engage with the texts through the lens of handling primary-source documents. On occasion, the curriculum preempts any move toward critical inquiry by the students, either by harmonizing texts that stand in tension with one another or by silently side-stepping the issue.[21] At key points, the BHL departs from analysis of the text altogether, employing, for example, the unit on the Sinai Covenant to make an apologetic argument for the Ten Commandments as foundational to the American legal system.

We should mention one final issue before turning to the rival BLP textbook. The National Council "curriculum" is more a chapter outline of biblical texts to cover in the class—often with the bare instruction to read aloud the text—than a coherent set of lesson plans. Worksheets supplied by the curriculum ask the student to rehearse information rather than to undertake any reflection on the text. The abundant use of simple read-aloud directives suggests that there is no programmatic goal for the course, other than to have the Bible read aloud in the school. It leads us to the conclusion that a central, albeit unstated, aim of the curriculum is to perform the authority of the Bible within the school in a manner that echoes, even as does the use of Proverbs in the curriculum, the pre-*Abington* exercises, albeit without the devotional trappings. We note also that there is a congruity between the designation of the Bible as a textbook and the customary exercise of reading aloud as the primary classroom activity: both are supported by a view that the Bible is a transparent text that immediately conveys its meaning to the student/reader. In both of these features, the curriculum not only fails to provide for critical interruption of any presupposed meanings for the text, its design forestalls opportunities for such interruption. The class, in such a case, simply becomes a forum in which the community can play out its own meanings without any interruption from external authorities. This runs afoul of our concerns stated in the previous chapter, for courses to avoid misrecognition and nonrecognition of potential members of its public.

This shortcoming manifests itself in the linear approach of the BHL, which limits the range of biblical investigation to a single, approved understanding. The BHL makes little or no effort to include diverse viewpoints in its curriculum. In fact, where points of diversity might emerge rather naturally, the NCBCPS makes an effort to block those avenues. The most notable example in this respect is the erasure of the Jewish tradition from the lesson plans on the Sinai Covenant, which are focused almost entirely on delineating a connection between the Ten Commandments and American law. Here it not only fails to enable students to understand that there are other perspectives—it actively obscures them from consideration.

THE BIBLE AND ITS INFLUENCE AS A CURRICULUM

The *Bible and Its Influence* develops a more comprehensive pedagogical experience than the read-aloud scheme outlined in *The Bible in History and Literature*. The textbook summarizes the content of each of the biblical books for students, including deuterocanonical material, supplemented by features that connect biblical literature to artistic representations, music, language, and science. The chapters provide numerous prompts for student writing and discussion, calling for synthesis of information, inference from narrative, and reflection on broader implications. The teacher's edition systematically instructs teachers on how to use the textbook in conjunction with a biblical text, with a blend of methodological and pedagogical techniques that move between moments of close textual analysis and broader thematic reflection, between teacher-directed discussion and cooperative student projects. In short, the BI is not simply a compendium of background information as an ancillary aid to the course; it maps out a thoroughly conceptualized classroom experience.

One of its most notable features, in comparison to the BHL, is the attention given to the contribution of the Bible to Jewish cultural identity. *The Bible and Its Influence* includes a chapter that orients students to the study of the Hebrew Bible. This chapter, which has no parallel in the rival National Council curriculum, is short on critical methodology for biblical study but rich in introducing a culturally Jewish Bible. The textbook chapter explains the origins of the acronym "Tanakh"—frequently used as shorthand for the three subdivisions of the Hebrew canon—offers a brief overview of Jewish exegetical tradition, includes visual representations of Jewish manuscript illumination, and lists the Hebrew names of the biblical books. The teacher is directed to rehearse this information in the classroom.

> Write on the board the terms *Torah, Nevi'im,* and *Ketuvim,* and circle the initial letters of the terms. Explain to students that Hebrew is usually written without vowels.... The acronym TNK in Hebrew is pronounced Tanakh.[22]

According to the teacher's guide, this distinctive canon should become visibly recognized in the classroom.

> Acknowledge that students coming from Christian traditions may find it difficult to detach themselves from that viewpoint when reading the Hebrew Scriptures, and may even consider the attempt to do so contrary to their faith . . . Remind students that this course concentrates on a nondevotional reading of the Bible, and encourage them to be as open to and respectful of multiple viewpoints as possible.[23]

The word "nondevotional" leaps out to us as particularly revealing here. Recall that Morris Black also insisted that his class accept this distinction as definitive of the course's operation. In his case, however, a "nondevotional" approach meant that the class strives to define the historical sequence of events to which the Bible bears witness. In this case, "nondevotional" means something else; it means that students accept the pluralism of the class, the religious other, as a necessary element of its investigation. In this way—and we could multiply the examples—the BI orchestrates classroom moments that establish the religious "other" as a visible entity in the classroom; the class becomes a means to make manifest a diverse public rather than function simply as an extension of a dominant community. It strives, in our terms, for recognition over nonrecognition.

The Bible and Its Influence reiterates these themes throughout the textbook. These points remind students that biblical interpretation takes place in situations that can be marked by conflict and challenge. In contrast to the National Council, *The Bible and Its Influence* includes the Jews as contemporary heirs of biblical tradition—not just as the "people of Israel" from whom biblical tradition descended.[24] The BLP, in contrast to the National Council curriculum, lifts up Torah as not only a historical past—the code of ancient Israel—but as a continuing and definitive component of contemporary Jewish identity. More broadly, the BLP provides the basis on which a student might see the meaning of the Bible as mediated through different communities and times. This adds a layer of thickness to the biblical text, alerting the student that he or she might not have an immediately transparent relationship to the text. This structure of the course situates the experience of the student within a context marked by tradition and difference, by disagreement and conflict. The study of the Bible is not a vehicle to reduce difference—social, intellectual, ethnic, cultural—to a single authoritative meaning.

The primary virtue of the BLP for public education, and it is no slight one, is its presentation of an array of hermeneutical perspectives on the Bible—most prominently, African-American Christian and Jewish readings and usage of the text.[25] It shows an approach to the Bible that is informed not simply by a variant exegesis, but that what readers encounter as "the Bible" is already shaped by their own cultural experience. This promotes an approach to the Bible that is culturally embedded, and the BLP in this way creates a textured classroom experience—one that does not simply seek to mirror the preconceptions of a student (and the sponsoring local community), but that rather enables the student to connect himself or herself to other readers. That is, the experience of reading the Bible under this framework could enable the student to recognize the strangers around herself as part of her "public." There are some clear limits to how far the BI extends this recognition. The curriculum more comfortably embraces religious traditions as defined by their conservative branches; it does not give much voice to critique—either internal or external—to religious traditions, of the ways in the Bible can be, and indeed has been, employed in the interests of power and the oppression of the marginalized.[26] One teacher, for example, whose school employed the BLP curriculum expressed dismay at a special feature in the BI that leveraged the Eden story to present traditional male-female marriage as the definitive biblical and natural practice (31–33). "Where will my gay students see themselves?" he asked us.

Without dismissing the significance of these limitations, we would judge this to be a matter of detail, which teachers of different inclinations could raise within the classroom. The overall effect remains that the BI strives to present the Bible as a text with multiple voices appropriated by multiple readers. The BLP, by presenting the Bible as a text jointly shared—and sometimes contested—by religious communities internalizes a measure of interruption within the structure of the curriculum. The National Council, on the other hand, projects an understanding of the Bible possessed by one religious community without interruption from any competing perspectives. The National Council does not appeal to open democratic values in its curriculum and holds that diversity is a source of the nation's educational problems. Chuck Norris, a spokesperson for the National Council, lambastes education standards that "whitewash the Judeo-Christian convictions of our founders."

Liberals and progressives complain that conservatives are hijacking the curriculum process and modifying textbooks to fit their ideological whims. But the history of textbook alterations has clearly proven it is the former who have changed the course and content of curricula and textbook production. Conservatives have been largely the guardians or preservationists of tradition. Progressives have changed curricula content to pacify the politically correct and adopt what they value today and want others to value tomorrow.[27]

For Norris and likeminded advocates of a Christian America, the Bible course opens another front in the culture war—a war that, in their view, they did not seek, but are morally bound to continue to its conclusion. *The Bible in History and Literature,* as an effort to embody that view, seeks to give as little ground as absolutely necessary to an educational establishment it sees as decadent and enthralled to progressive and secular interests. The National Council sees the significance of the Bible course as, in part, giving a voice to a constituency—and not any constituency, but the preservers of the spirit of the Founders—that, in its view, has deliberately and pervasively been silenced. It is not incumbent upon them, consequently, to represent "diversity" within this course; it is rather the secular forces wielding the shibboleth of "diversity" that have silenced the religious vision of America in the first place.

This narrative is deeply ironic. The National Council and its allies represent themselves as preserving the one true vision of American identity, but seize upon the rhetoric of the marginalized and the outsider to secure "rights" in the public arena. The National Council simultaneously laments the *Abington* decision as the exclusion of God from the public schools and relies on that same opinion as unimpeachable justification for the constitutionality of its curriculum. Irony aside, all this suggests that the failure to conform to principles we have identified as foundational to a humanities model of education is not a shortcoming in the execution of the project, but part and parcel of its design and appeal.

BACK TO JORDAN COUNTY: IMPLEMENTING *THE BIBLE AND ITS INFLUENCE*

Sam Watson may not have undertaken such a detailed comparison when he selected the BLP textbook and teacher's guide. The factors he took into consideration, however, placed a premium on the criterion of recognition. He told us that he appreciated the high level of support and training BLP offered in conjunction with the use of its textbook, and he was swayed by the support the project drew from a wide swath of constituencies. He expressed to us that he was impressed with:

> How rigorous they were in screening this textbook. They checked with the ACLU, B'nai B'rith, various civil liberties groups, religious groups, in order to make sure that what they were producing achieved their goal of emphasizing the impact the Bible's had without treading on any gray areas—or even black

areas—of things that groups opposed on a legal basis, of church-state issues. And I was impressed with how thorough they were in that.

Watson's regard for the imprimatur of such groups reflects, as we take it at least, an aim for a course that enables a public to emerge through the mutual recognition of communities of tradition. He closely follows the textbook in his syllabus. Probing more deeply, one of the differences that struck us between Ridge and Jordan is the extent to which educational, rather than just legal, considerations controlled discussion of *how* to structure and teach the Jordan class. While Ballard was certainly concerned about constitutional matters, Mr. Watson's focus was on the educational significance of the course and its potential to extend the student's understanding of their time and culture in light of the past. He did suspect that he was asked to teach the course because he was known to be a churchgoing Christian, but, as we mentioned earlier, he thought that might serve as much as a liability as an asset. He does hold that his identity as a Christian provides him with a sympathetic relationship to both the subject and his believing students, but he was also concerned that his reputation as a religious person could prompt students to steer the course in a religious, rather than an academic, direction. It is an asset because of his knowledge of the Bible. It is a liability because, as he puts it:

> As a public school teacher for seventeen years, I was aware of the kinds of things you can and cannot say. But as a Christian my concern is that I not slip into a Sunday school teacher mode. It would be very easy to do that because I think a lot of kids in this class are churched kids and many know the stories of the Bible and some are pretty devout Christians, so the class could lead into that grey area of advocating rather than studying from an academic level.

He worries that his affinity with the devout Christian students could undermine the academic mission of the course, turning it into a "testimonial for Jesus."

It is worth noting that Watson, like Morris Black, is keenly aware of constitutional issues. There is, however, a subtle, but significant difference. Black experiences the constitutional mandates as an external constraint—a threat looming over the class like an ACLU lawyer prepared to pounce on any transgression. For Watson, the constitutional principles correspond with his own educational aims, framed less as governmental neutrality than as a hope to use the classroom to broaden the forum in which students see themselves as civic actors. He fore-sees possible situations where his reputation as a committed Christian could inhibit the achievement of this aim.

Watson employs the BLP, and sometimes expands on it, to alert students to a variety of diversities in the Bible. For instance, he dwells in class upon the BI's brief discussion of the construction of the canon (208–9). In highlighting the canonization process he brings to view not just the factors internal to the Chris-tian community (as the BLP presentation does), but also includes some of the political factors that went into its making. He describes this discussion to us:

> (The class) talked about process and how certain groups accepted some books and other groups accepted other books. That raised some questions about why certain groups accept these and why others don't have them, particularly for these students the things they wouldn't agree with, the apocrypha—sometimes called the Catholic Bible versus the Protestant Bible—and why those deu-terocanonical books are included in the Catholic and not the Protestant. I just wanted them to understand some of the process with certain groups meeting and voting on certain books and their inclusion or not.

This foregrounding of social and political imprints on the shape of the Chris-tian Bible establishes a very different metanarrative from the one fostered by Morris Black's Bible History class. Watson brackets the status of the Bible as a sacred object in order to focus on the process of construction. He does not draw any conclusion about the divine origins of the Bible. Rather, he provides students with information that will help them to develop their own ideas, and displays some of the multiple ways in which Christianity has been expressed, often using locally available religious groups, both contemporary and historical, to illustrate this diversity.

Besides teaching about different understandings of Christianity, he also challenges standard interpretations of religious parables in an effort to promote reflection and critical thinking about fairness. Here is an example from the par-able of the prodigal son.

> I asked them about the older brother, and I told them that for me personally, it has always been intriguing, looking at that character in the story, and I asked them if they could relate to the older brother, and if so, in what way. And after some questioning and some back and forth, some of the students said that yeah,

they've been in situations where they've done the work, they've toed the line, they've done everything they are supposed to be doing, and then someone else who's not, who's a slacker or whatever else the distinction might be, they're being rewarded. They could see some divergent views on what the meaning of it was. And whether or not the other brother's action was correct, being able to understand and relate to it and having to deal with that.

In contrast to the teachers at Ridge County, he does not present the Bible as a transparent text. While this problematizing of the parable would be at home even in a mainline Protestant sermon—it would scarcely be a shocking departure from traditional piety—it nevertheless nudges the students to seeing the Bible as a text to be "investigated," to use the California Social Studies Association terminology. In contrast to Mr. Black, who was concerned not to raise issues that might lead students to doubt their religious beliefs, Mr. Watson tells us that he is not concerned if his classes led some students to question their religion. He draws a line in initiating discussions that could be divisive within the class. Watson identifies the doctrine of purgatory as an instance of a topic he would introduce gingerly, if at all.

To this point, then, we have seen that the Bible course at Jordan begins with some of the same concerns for conveying a sense of moral order as we saw at Ridge. As the course planning progressed, however—from the school board president to the superintendent, to the principal and then the teacher— its rationale also changed. The perceived character of the moral order shifted from that of a timeless code, toward which obedience is required, to a literary and rhetorical tradition which can find diverse expressions. The metanarrative underlying the course likewise shifted, from a validation of the Bible as a transparent witness to historical events to a Bible that has been shaped by the communities that use it. In keeping with this, the totalizing vision of Ridge's Bible History class gives way to one that prizes broader recognition. It is in this last goal that Watson innovates most notably on the BLP curriculum, and as we will see shortly, it also induces greater distress for him when this standard is not met.

THE BEST-LAID PLANS: THE LORD'S HARVEST COMES TO JORDAN HIGH

In introducing students to some of the diverse ways that the Bible is used and understood, Watson hopes to communicate to the students that the Bible is a living resource for diverse populations in Jordan County itself, that it can support different visions of the civic good. Mr. Watson frequently uses local outside sources to help students understand how the Bible works in people's everyday lives. He takes students on field trips to religious communities in the surrounding region, including the nearest synagogue, and invites speakers into his class. As Watson summarized his understanding of the curriculum:

> The way I look at the curriculum is the impact that the Bible has had on "X." And X could be styles of literature; it could be on historical movements. And it could be music, and it could be a lot of different areas. And one area, one of those major areas I see, would be social causes.

This aim shapes the entire trajectory of the yearlong course. For example, in the opening exercise for the course, Watson divides students into small groups that develop reports on utopian communities of the past and present that have used the picture of the early Christian community in the Book of Acts "as a model to create their own society." The latter part of the course included a visit from an AIDS activist arguing for a biblical foundation to address the international epidemic of children living in the shadow of the disease. The aim of these guest spots in the course is to make students more aware of the varieties of religious experience within their own community. The events can be highly rewarding, but giving up control of the class can also be risky.

By far, the most electric event for the class the year we observed was the guest presentation by Doug Mason, director of Lord's Harvest, a local Christian prison ministry. The visit took place on a sticky late-May afternoon, when the seniors in the classroom had already turned their attention more to graduation and its parties than to coursework. Watson confessed to us that the timing of the visit was not ideal, as the annual Senior Day picnic preempted class the next day, with the result that he would not have the opportunity to review the session with students. Despite the competition from these year-end events, a nervous twitter replaced the usual idle chatter in the room as Mason patiently waited in front of the blackboard, along with two other men, before class began. Mason, dressed casually in khakis and a button-down shirt, appeared comfortable with the audience. His companions, clad in frayed jeans and t-shirts, faces marked by deep creases and stubble, were clearly nervous.

After a brief overview of the scope of Lord's Harvest's ministry, Mason turned to his main argument, which advanced a case for a faith-based approach to substance-abuse treatment. Mason strictly distinguished a "biblical" from a "secular" explanation for addiction, framed in terms of a "choice model" versus a "disease model." He further identified the biblical theory of addiction as a result of a sequence of choices reinforced over time—that is, as a voluntarily induced habit. This theory places addiction within the category of "sin" rather than that of disease. Mason continued to specify the nature of that sin; in what follows we provide some substantial excerpts to convey the flavor of the talk as experienced by the students.

> There are a number of themes that we use to try to address the substance addiction issue. One of the ones we use very often is the basic Old Testament and New Testament declaration that Jesus is Lord. Meaning that he's our master, he's the one that we are to love, to serve, to obey. And we kind of attack the addiction issue that we're bowing down to a different Lord. We're serving, and obeying, and trusting, and loving a different master, a different Lord, than our Creator Lord.

> We use the category of idolatry to talk about addiction. Addiction is really a worship issue: who will I serve, who will I love, who will I depend on and trust? We go to our substances, we go to our addictions that we struggle with because we want something from them. And in essence, we're saying "You're my god. Help me! Deliver me! Give me some kind of payoff."

> One more thing that we use very much from the Scripture is the Psalms. The Psalms is a prayer book in the middle of your Bible. And it's 150 songs of real life people who are facing difficult stuff, and they struggle with fear, they struggle with worry and doubt, they get angry, but then they remember God, and his promises and his character, and as they focus on God, their faith begins to get strong again. This one simple verse will illustrate how we use this in our program, a verse like Psalm 16:1, "Preserve me, O God." This is King David writing this. "Preserve me, O God, for you I take refuge." What we picture the addiction issue as I'm taking refuge in a false refuge. I'm fleeing to what I think is a place of safety and power and comfort, but it turns out to stab me in the back sooner or later. Whereas we use the Bible to introduce us to God and learn that He's my refuge and the goal is that we flee consistently to God, to Jesus instead of fleeing to the false refuge of substance.

As can be seen from these quotations, Mason leverages diverse biblical quotations without reference to their textual or historical context; they are oracles of timeless truth concerning the nature of human weakness. The basic contention is that addiction can only be fully addressed as a symptom of a deeper sin—the sin of idolatry. Those who suffer from addiction do so because they bring false hope to their use of substances; that it will provide a "refuge" from their problems. The remedy for addiction begins, consequently, with the removal of this "false god" and the submission of the addict to the true Lord, Jesus Christ. This general theory of addiction also contains the seeds of Mason's own pitch for the class.

> Stats really say that when you compare a faith-based program like ours with secular rehabs, that the success rate—meaning they don't continue to return to the addictions—faith-based has about a 70 percent success rate and secular rehabs have about a 30 percent success rate. That's just a fact. And so people in the government started to look at that and say "Wow! Seventy percent do well here and thirty percent do well here, maybe we should shift some of our monies into faith-based."

Mason makes sweeping claims about the effectiveness of faith-based addiction treatments that are difficult to probe in the classroom setting. Before this point in the yearlong course, the students have not had any exposure to theories of addiction or its treatment, so the class is not well prepared to consider this dimension of the presentation. As a class on Bible, however, Mason makes a number of statements that would be flirting with constitutional boundaries were a teacher to make them. For instance, he states without qualification that the "Old Testament" and New Testament both declare that "Jesus is Lord," narrowing the usage of the Hebrew Scriptures to a Christian viewpoint. He rhetorically shapes the class as a whole into a congregation of believers, telling them that the Psalms is in the middle of "your Bible" and collapsing any distance between Lord's Harvest and the class itself: "we use the Bible to introduce us to God and learn that He's my refuge and the goal is that we flee consistently to God, to Jesus instead of fleeing to the false refuge of substance."

Such statements place Watson himself in a delicate position: does he have a responsibility to distance the school—the sponsor of the visit—from these assertions, or is it enough simply not to reinforce them? He is caught between the duties of hospitality to an invited guest and the duty of maintaining neutrality with respect to religion. Mason's presentation, and its advocacy for the claims of faith-based interventions, did not rest on cool logic. Students listened politely to his speech, which integrated modern therapeutic discourse with a traditional, revivalist call for transformation. The students were rapt with attention, however, for what followed. Mason introduced the two men who accompanied him as two former prisoners, Mike and Jerry. Both were then participants in the Lord's Harvest post–release program. Both then gave ten-minute testimonials illustrating the transformative power that Mason had claimed for his ministry. Both had dropped out of high school, and had slipped into more serious criminal activity, and both told the class that Bible study had saved them. Each admitted he had suffered relapses in his journey, but the relapses had produced a clearer sense of his addiction and the need he had to rely on Jesus alone.

Students fixed each of the men with their whole gaze, some of their eyes glistening with tears. They broke into laughter at their self-deprecating humor and applause at the conclusion of each testimonial. Each testimonial concluded with a selection of Bible passages each man found particularly relevant to his own situation. Jerry quoted from 2 Corinthians and expressed its significance to himself: "it opened my eyes that I am worthy of forgiveness, that in Christ I get a second chance." It was this verse, he said, that "started to break down the idea that I was unworthy." He read a lengthy passage from Romans 7, to the effect that Paul found himself doing "not what I want but I do the very thing I hate." There are many ways to look at this verse, he said, "but as an addict, I looked at it and this is my life, you know, this is how I lived my life." The voice of Paul was, for this man, a direct mirror of his own life, and he presented it to the class as a mirror for their own lives as well. He brought his speech to a close with the warning that "anything that comes between you and God" is idolatry and that in "the world we live in today, you got more coming between us and God than ever before."

The content of Mason's *argument* for a faith-based approach to substance abuse as a biblical mandate was overshadowed for the students by the sheer experience of watching redemption in action. Both men presented themselves as in the middle of a continuing journey, for which their daily practices of Scripture reading were essential supports. Each concluded by sharing some passages from the Bible that were particularly significant to them. They presented these passages as having direct, unmediated relevance to their own lives. These heartfelt testimonies connected with the students in a direct way—from the boyish discomfort of the men as they found themselves in a school room to the artless manner of their presentation, to the direct, uncritical appropriation of biblical words—the transformation of their lives was the proof of the Scriptures, and, more concretely, proof of the truth of Lord's Harvest.

This experience was thick, complex, and multilayered, and would have required much time and careful planning for Mr. Watson to unpack with his class. It brought home to us as observers that guest presentations engage students at several levels and it is hazardous to predict what students would take home from the experience—they might not even be able to articulate what they learned. Even if students did not absorb Mason's argument for faith-based approach to addiction treatment, they exhibited an emotional response to the broader unstated claim: only belief can truly transform a person, and belief can come only through the Scriptures. The men were palpable demonstrations of this claim. The message of the men of discovering that "God still loved me" carried a powerful appeal to the students, speaking to their desire to be integrated into a community, to have a place and acceptance.

ASSESSING LORD'S HARVEST: A TEACHER'S REFLECTION

This was a single classroom session in the flow of a long, full-year program. It spotlighted, however, some of the most interesting issues we could imagine. One might regard this as skirting constitutional lines. The testimonials clearly advanced a view that salvation is only possible through Jesus Christ, but the context in which the testimonials entered the classroom was defined by the self-understanding of the Lord's Harvest Ministry. The speakers were there to represent *their own worldview,* and the use of other speakers in the semester might be advanced as evidence that the school did not endorse any single visitor's view.

When he spoke to us after the prison-ministry class was over, Mr. Watson was not happy, and was indeed somewhat apologetic. Watson entered into this event with a clear idea of the rationale for the visit. A previous visit had come from a group leaning to the left, politically speaking—the AIDS relief organization. Lord's Harvest would, in his view, balance the curriculum by exposing students to a group more associated with conservative political values. He viewed the two visits as bookends, which both provided a balance, and also, more broadly, exposed students to the ways in which the Bible can inform social values and programs across a broad political spectrum, and indeed does so right within their community.

That is, Mr. Watson approached the slate of field trips and visits from a perspective of equal time for competing views. The teacher's role in this case was to structure a set of experiences that did not endorse any single view and allowed multiple and diverse perspectives on the Bible and its role in shaping these particular organizations to be brought before the students. From a perspective of constitutional legitimacy, this seems defensible, even if striving to provide equal access is not identical to neutrality. Even at this level, however, the Lord's Harvest visit induced a few butterflies for Watson.

> [Q]: I'll ask the question this way: do you think any of the students could have perceived their presentation today as testimonial?
> [A]: Yes. [brief pause] The first gentleman who spoke, who works for the prison ministry, Mr. Mason, that's what I had in mind when I contacted the ministry about having someone come in and talking. And then he suggested bringing in a couple of the men in the ministry and to give firsthand. And when they spoke, that was more of a testimonial than what I was thinking of. So, as they were talking, my teacher-here-at-the school-mind, I'm thinking "I think this is OK, but this is probably one of those areas" that it's a fine line and, cause I was thinking, "Now if the principal was in here at the moment what would he say?"
> [Q]: And what do you think he would say?
> [A]: I think he would probably at least have some reservations, or red flags. I don't know that he necessarily would say, "That's over the limit, that's not allowed."

Mr. Watson's reflection here indicates, most obviously, that this particular visit came too close for comfort to the constitutional boundaries as he understood them. It also points more generally to the complexities a teacher faces in dealing with outside groups. It was not his idea to include the "firsthand" experiences of Mike and Jerry. This was a suggestion by Mason and accorded more with the interests of Lord's Harvest than the purpose of the visit as Watson initially conceived it. He lost some measure of control over the event when he allowed Doug Mason to extend the original invitation to the other participants. Yet, it was Mike and Jerry's talk that provided the transformational force for the event—that moved the experience from being about an approach to addiction to being an encounter with a transformed person.

One of the issues it presents for a teacher is the manner in which it erases the difference in how one talks about biblical texts, eschewing the discourse of the classroom for the vocabulary of the church. All three presenters referred to the Bible as the "Scriptures," adopting the perspective of those internal to the believing community. The students responded emotionally—as their laughter, tears, and applause indicate—before they grasped the mechanisms that caused that response. The question then becomes "what kind of pedagogical context will best advance the students ability to interpret this experience?" rather than "is this a valid educational experience?"

Our discussion centered around whether, without proper preparation, the exercise had a legitimate place in the classroom, and it became clear to us that Mr. Watson has an implicit notion about what is and what is not educationally appropriate. As he reflected on the presentation, he began to see the need for follow-up discussion of the event: "As they were talking I began to have concerns. I see it as needing to follow up afterwards with a discussion." He compared the Lord's Harvest presentation to a field trip early in the year to a Mennonite religious community that had constructed a model of Israel's tabernacle. At that time, Watson coached the students in advance that the members of that community would convey their own religious views, and that the students should respect them accordingly. Extrapolating from that experience, Watson judged:

> And I think that with the juniors and seniors in class, their age level, and the way that we have earlier in the year talked about the issues of church and state and me preparing them and telling them how I see the course, I think they would be able to see that as "yes, that's that person's testimony" and not feel if they don't agree with it or don't feel receptive that they're being threatened or they're being pushed. That's how I see it. I don't know if I'm right or not, but that's my initial reaction.

Watson's justification for the presentation incorporates two main points: (1) the age and maturity of the students, and (2) the context created by the course as a whole. Students with the requisite maturity should be able to fold this experience into the wider horizons of the diversity of the course as a whole. He believes that in choosing speakers he needs to consider the makeup of the local community—its concerns, culture, and expectations—and he needs to provide some balance to his invited speakers. In addition, he needs to help prepare the students by reminding them that this is an academic context, and that they are hearing people with different ideas and from different perspectives. He acknowledges that there can be a problem for students in distinguishing between the teacher as facilitating the expression of certain perspectives and the teacher as endorsing a given perspective, and he allows that students could come away with the view that a certain speaker had a special authority to speak about the truth of the Bible. In other words, for a presentation to be educationally valuable he believes that students need to be provided with "different kinds of presentations and balancing experiences."

From our perspective, however, Watson's reflection missed one important point. Not all presentations or guest speakers present the same form of challenge. He was primarily concerned about students who might feel "threatened" or "offended" by the presentation. As we were observing the class, however, the chief danger was quite the reverse. The chief difficulty was that this revival-laden rhetoric is fully consistent with the students' own experience. This congruence between the guest's language and the student's experience complicates the ability of the teacher to maintain any kind of mediating distance from the event.

A LIBERAL VIEW: MEDIATION AS EDUCATION

Watson felt that, problematic as it was, the prison ministry was acceptable when placed in the context of all of the other classes because he believed that together they exposed the students to a range of diverse ways of using the Bible. His goal of exposing students to this diversity fits nicely into our understanding of the defining role of a public education. It suggests that students need to see that the Bible is situated in communities, that there are different ways to appropriate it, and that, in contrast to Ridge, it is not just to be understood as one master book of moral rules. Exposing students to religious diversity allows them to see that there are different ways of appropriating a text and it brings them into contact with strangers: either real—in the case of the prison ministry, or vicarious—through texts and virtual experiences. Moreover, it provides opportunities to acknowledge the stranger and to engage emotionally with other ways of life, and in doing so it might provide the conditions for students to reflect upon their own ways of life—although we did not see this happen in Watson's class. And, in the case of the prison ministry, as well as the AIDS ministry that he sees as its balance, Watson is clearly engaging students with strangers, with people that they could not be expected to run across in their everyday lives. But there is something missing in these encounters.

The prisoners are acknowledged not because of their religious strangeness but because of their religious similarities to the students. This and the AIDS ministry provide an instance where strangeness is dissolved by sameness. Both depend on the presumptions familiar to this evangelical community about the saving power of Jesus and about the possibilities Christianity provides for self-transformation. In both cases, strangeness is dissolved and we have what Hegel called the night where all cows are black.

In this respect, Watson's understanding of neutrality as equal representation is flawed. Representation that reinforces a student's worldview without providing the tools and information to reflect upon and evaluate it cannot be counted as *educational* neutrality. Educational neutrality requires mediation between the views presented and the students' emotional response to them. In this case, it would have required that the teacher use the presentations to provide the students the skills required to compare and contrast them and to evaluate the social claims that they may make. In the next chapter, we turn to a teacher and a form of Bible course that attempts to develop these requisite skills.

Chapter 6

THE BIBLE AS LITERATURE
Detachment as a Means toward Autonomy

Before they are subjects to be studied, the humanities are practices to be engaged in—practices that produce, perpetuate, and reproduce human communities. One important task of the humanities *as curricular subjects* is to enable students to *recognize* themselves as embedded, often through canonical texts, in particular human communities. However, another equally important task for the humanities is to prepare students to engage with new communities and to develop the interpretive, analytic, and critical skills that intelligent engagement requires. The construction of a public, an association of strangers, requires that along with these skills students develop a disposition for self-reflection and thus come to see both themselves and strangers as embedded in meaningful but fluid traditions. Conservatives are not unreasonable when they suggest that the failure to teach about the Bible in the public schools ignores a critical source for meaning making. Yet they are amiss if they fail to understand that to teach the Bible as if its meaning were set in stone, fixed and absolute, is to deny to students active agency in the construction of meaning and to minimize their role as coconstructors of a renewing public.

Bible courses that promote the construction of civic publics can develop interpretive skills, provide students with the opportunity to shape meaning, and develop student self-awareness as agents in public renewal. These courses require teachers who understand that many students already have emotional investments in religious ideas and that these investments influence the way they understand the world and their views about other religions. Three different kinds of capacities are important if students are to understand themselves as interpretive agents. First, it requires an awareness that an object or a text *calls* for interpretation and is not just there as a conduit to have its content delivered unchanged. Second, it requires critical reading skills where the student reflects on and responds to traditional texts, whether or not he or she accepts them. Finally, it requires that students begin to see their own traditions as embracing multiple possibilities. In this chapter, we provide an illustration of the way these skills might be developed in a Bible course.

READING FOR MEANING

Interpretation is the process of giving meaning to experiences by making connections, seeing relationships, and assigning categories. Interpretation is something that goes on all the time and is involved in the seemingly most simple of activities. We see a red, hard, smooth, round object as an apple because we are able to bring color, level of resistance, texture, and shape together and subsume it under existing categories—apples, good to eat. We could also ignore the redness and subsume it under the category of things that are good to throw, or in the case of Isaac Newton, to drop and measure the rate of fall. Usually we do not think of everyday seeing as an interpretive act, but much of modern art is designed to make us conscious of our acts of interpretation—for example, Magritte's *This is not a Pipe*.

One of the tasks of a citizen in a democracy is to be sensitive to the way in which interpretations, both his or her own and those of others, are built up. One of the tasks of a humanities course is to provide students with opportunities to become aware of and to interrogate their own interpretive framework. This is a controversial goal where religion is concerned. Indeed, in the previous chapters we have seen teachers who believe that they can maintain their neutrality by avoiding any interpretive slant and by just reading it "like it is." This desire to read it like it is and to avoid the appearance of interpretation rests on an important moral concern that needs to be acknowledged. These teachers are concerned that what they see as "interpretation" invites arbitrary opinions into the reading of the texts. At the same time they fail to understand that the very idea that one can "read it like it is" implicitly adopts a "Protestant" view that the meaning of the Bible is transparent and is there for all to see.[1] These teachers wrongly believe that when taught in this way, the Bible course allows space for all kinds of belief or nonbelief, while in fact the teacher is actually promoting one way of thinking about the Bible over others. In Bible History courses, students typically are not informed of the multiple ways in which the Bible is understood in different interpretive communities. By not informing students of the different ways in which readers approach the Bible, the teacher quite arbitrarily reinforces the standpoint of certain readers while not recognizing that of others, thus failing to meet one of our floor considerations: the responsibility to avoid nonrecognition.

This is arguably acceptable for a religious school in a pluralistic democracy but is extremely problematic for a public one. An alternative is not to deny the value of what is called "a literal reading" of the Bible but to show how any reading—literal or not—has an interpretive element. Yet, by consciously engaging students in an interpretive inquiry about their own religious understandings, we move beyond the inside views developed in early religious socialization and begin to engage the perspective of the outsider. We are teaching students to be aware of themselves as participants in meaning making.

TEACHING FOR MEANING AT LAKESIDE HIGH

Donna Smith teaches the Bible as Literature elective class at Lakeside High School. Lakeside High is located in the suburban community of Lake City, a lengthy commute from a major urban center. Administrators at the school describe Lakeside as having a small-town feel, but due to rapid urban sprawl and an increase in local industry the small city is gradually being transformed into a suburban community of about 30,000 people. The median household income of Lake City has grown significantly from $69,000 to $91,000 before the recent recession, signaling the growing suburbanization of the area. In fact, in ten years the high school underwent two massive expansion projects in order to accommodate the city's increasing population. While typical of many communities drawn into the suburban net, Lake City differs from the other areas we studied in that it is more religiously diverse with a large Catholic population, in addition to a Protestant one, and access to a mosque and synagogue in neighboring towns.

At Lakeside, the Bible course is sponsored by the English department and is marketed to the students and their parents as a Bible literacy course, with the goal of helping students better to understand the Bible as an important literary text, not a historical or social text. Even though the department highlights biblical literacy as improving a student's collegiate prospects, Ms. Smith tells us that only a small minority of her Bible students harbor ambitions to obtain degrees from four-year institutions. Her Bible as Literature class imparts skills for citizenship, but is promoted for enhancing individual achievement. Ms. Smith does not claim to be a biblical scholar and tells her students that she does not have a strong religious background. Unlike Mr. Milsap, who was fired up to teach his course, she inherited the course from a retiring teacher and was not all that comfortable with the legacy. She worries that parents might feel threatened. Nevertheless, through a combination of humility, diplomacy, and respect for community sensitivities, she feels she has managed to gain legitimacy in their eyes—or at least to avoid overt resistance.

The course includes elements from both the Hebrew Bible, which Ms. Smith refers to, without commentary, as the "Old Testament" and the New Testament. Ms. Smith brackets for the students the question of the truth of biblical stories and encourages the students to explore them for their literary qualities by using literary rather than historical categories. She refers to the episodes as *stories*, the people as *characters*, and raises questions about plot, narrative completeness, and character development. The relevant questions for this class are not whether the Bible is true, or what the Bible can teach us, or what moral lessons the Bible provides. They are about plot, structure, and character. As Ms. Smith tells one of the parents: "This is not a religion class"; this course teaches the same skills as would "any other English class"—that is, writing skills and reading skills. She also tells parents that the course is helpful for reading literary classics, such as Shakespeare, and for college applications. However, as we will see, the class has more than utilitarian value.

CRITICAL REFLECTION

Smith begins her class by explaining to the students the way in which the Bible differs from other literature. "The Bible," she tells her students, "is filled with bits and pieces and that there may be parts missing." To illustrate this she has the student do a puzzle facedown, and when it is over the students discover that their completed puzzle didn't really match the picture on the box. Smith used this exercise to discuss the problem scholars have in reconstructing the fragmentary Dead Sea Scrolls. Then she cautions the students, "there's going to be questions raised when reading these stories. We don't know what everything exactly means. Ideas are vague and missing and they just aren't going to have the answers. Do we need to know everything to get the basics of the story?"

To allow the students to hear that ideas are vague and some elements of the story are missing is to introduce them to the possibility that the meaning of the Bible is open to interpretation. Unlike Mr. Black and Mr. Milsap, who felt that they had to have all of the answers to their students' questions, Ms. Smith often tells her students that she just does not have the answer to their question and that they need to search it out together. She tells them:

> It's not like looking at a regular story; there are things missing. It's like an incomplete text. We don't know why things are missing. We can talk about what's missing but I can't fill in the blanks for you.

Smith frequently introduces a discussion by bringing her own reading problem to the class. Here's where I'm having a problem with Esther, she might begin: is it okay for a hero to practice deception? If Esther's deception is to be approved, why is her action judged differently from Jacob's? This kind of interrogative opening shifts the authority of the classroom away from the teacher to the entirety of the class. The task of the class is to consider questions rather than to produce definitive answers. Those questions can lead in unanticipated directions. For instance, when we attended the session on the Book of Esther, a student interrupted the discussion to ask a classic historical question: is the king of Persia in the narrative, referred to as Ahasuerus, a real person or not? Is the story of Esther "true" in the historical sense? Ms. Smith surprised us by suddenly including us—the silent observers—in discussing the issue. "Let's ask the experts," she declared. "What would *you* say?" We responded by turning the question back. "We'll give you our opinion," we replied, "but first let us ask you a question: What difference would it make to how you understand this story?" That question set off a lively debate among the students on the difference between the "meaning" and the "truth" of a narrative. The debate was lively enough that the students forgot at the end to ask our opinion.

This incident was remarkable for a number of reasons, not least for reflecting the collaborative approach to teaching that Ms. Smith favors. Beyond the pedagogical technique, however, it centers the work of the classroom on the open-ended question of meaning rather than on the mastery of content. She was constantly cultivating a spirit of inquiry in the classroom, while striving to respect her students' beliefs. For instance, she showed the students the documentary from the Discovery channel, *Noah's Ark: The True Story*. The program asked whether the well-known story was "fact." It raised a number of points that questioned the account from the perspective of "science," including whether it was possible to build a seaworthy vessel conforming to the biblical description, whether evidence of a global flood exists, and whether the reported vessel had the capacity to hold all the animals claimed. The film, Ms. Smith insisted, did not say that the ark story was itself not possible, only that modern science raises questions about a number of features of the story. By employing the film, however, the teacher was able to shape the classroom discussion as an inquiry about the relationship of faith to reason: what value, she asked, could or should scientific proof have for a matter of faith? In this way, the flood story provided an *occasion* for discussion of an issue that resonated with students, but did so in a manner that did not force a student to defend or deny the historicity of the biblical account itself. The documentary deflected the discussion to a second level—away from the text itself and onto broader cultural questions. By triangulating the issue in this manner, Ms. Smith aimed to enable students to flex critical muscles without requiring them directly to question an authoritative text. The operative question is not "is the flood story true?," but "what does the story mean for my view of issue X?"

Mrs. Smith initially reported to us that the exercise went quite well, stimulating a good discussion, she thought, about the nature of science and faith. A little bit later, however, on the day before the school's open house, a student pulled her aside after class to let her know the film put him in an awkward position at home. As she related the incident to us:

> I had one student after class today said he can't talk to his parents about that Noah's Ark movie that I showed because it would just be like "blaspheme." So that kind of made me kind of a little unnervy. He said, "I don't believe that. I see what they're trying to do, but I don't know if my parents would see it that way. So I don't know." So I said, "We're just trying to get you to think critically."

"It scares the heck of out me," she confessed, anxiously anticipating meeting the student's parents at the upcoming open house. All went well that evening, she later reported. It suggests to us that Ms. Smith deliberately pushes the critical and reflective dimensions to what she sees as the maximum weight the class can bear. The potential rewards of such an approach are manifest: to the extent that the Bible is a part of their own tradition, they have an opportunity to engage in *reflective* critical thinking and to see why the public they share in the classroom can hold highly different views of the same text.

We emphasize the word *reflective* as a modifier for critical thinking. While critical thinking is an accepted goal of education, it can mean many different things. To some, it simply means the ability to evaluate the logic of an argument and to determine whether the conclusions follow from the premises. Here, vagueness, ambiguity, clarity are all important targets of inquiry and the object can be any kind of discursive text, but usually one in which an argument is embedded, explicitly or implicitly. This notion of critical thinking is not itself reflective. To some theorists, critical thinking involves an awareness of one's immediate surroundings and how it conditions someone's beliefs and behavior. Yet unless this awareness is applied to oneself, it is not reflective. Still, other theorists identify critical thinking with acts of resistance against the pervasive influence of capitalism. Here critical thinking becomes a weapon in the cause of social justice, but it is social justice *as* the critic understands it and runs a risk of dogma or indoctrination. Each of these understandings has its limitations. One is too cold, abstract, and distant; another is too subjective or ideological.

The Bible is not an abstract or distant text; it is a direct or indirect part of many students' lives. Hence, to develop the capacity for detachment and the critical skills that go along with it students must learn to reflect on an important aspect of their own identity. Some schools will reserve courses like these for honor students, or, at the very least, for college-bound ones. This is not the case with Smith's students, who are a reasonably representative of the student body as a whole. Neither the heterogeneity of the class nor the religious background of many of her students is a reason to avoid developing reflective critical-thinking skills. Smith considers this as an integral part of her purpose.

> To get them to think critically about this, they have to get a paradigm shift. You can't change their belief system, but I think you have to get them to think beyond what they've been taught throughout their life. Asking them to look at the logical aspect of it. We talk about logical progression with the creation stories and Adam and Eve. How does this stuff fit in the story? You have to ask

students to put their belief system aside at some point and look at some of this stuff critically and rationally.

Smith understands that many of the students hear these stories in church and she does not feel that she is either reinforcing this experience or challenging it. To look at these stories critically does not entail judging their truth or falsity. It means exploring their nuances and complexity.

> They go to church and Sunday school and get one little snippet of a story, but when they get older they can start looking at some of the complexities of the stories and can see that there's more going on and that they're a little more complex. They come in with basic knowledge, but I want to see them struggle more with the nuances. They have to look at their belief systems to be critical. But it's scary and maybe I could get fired next year. (Laughter) But the kids are very good and we have a rapport and if there was an issue they'd let me know. They think it's interesting, what we're doing. They're open to what we're doing.

The remark about getting fired next year is meant as a joke, but she is aware of community sentiments and wants to respect them. Nevertheless, Smith is encouraging detachment and distance, even though she is not engaged in openly challenging her students' beliefs. To speak of creation as a story rather than an event in history allows her to talk about Adam and Eve as "characters." She can then look at them as archetypes, comparing them at times to the heroes and gods of Greek literature, while leaving the question whether they were also real people open for students to determine for themselves. To say that they are *characters* is not to say that they were not real people as well. However, it is not to claim that they were real people either. Characters like Samuel and Saul can serve as archetypes that magnify human virtues and fragilities and students then examine the biblical text along with relevant secondary sources. As students research the traits of different biblical characters, they expand their basic understanding of key biblical ideas by using secondary sources in addition to primary ones, and they seek out alternative meanings as they relate the stories to their own experience. Ms. Smith's advice to her students follows the canons of the mid-twentieth century New Criticism model, which may have limits, but opens up the students to a new kind of reading experience.

We tell the kids you can come up with your own ideas based on what the story has, but you can't, unless the author is alive and you can ask him, you can't really look at what the intention was for writing this. So we look at it more at face value, the book is what you have to work with. Come up with your ideas and defend your reasoning.

Contemporary literary critics might chafe at the implied notion here that a present-day author can grant the reader a privileged access to the text. In our view, however, there is a significant educational benefit to Smith's gentle prodding. Smith detaches students from the idea that the Bible offers a transparent window to ancient events and that the "intention" of the text is readily accessible. Smith's message is that the Bible is an interpretable document. Yes, we might take it at face value, but his does not mean that we must stay on the surface. Smith is telling her students: we must stay on the surface because the surface is all that is left of these otherwise fragmented parts. We do not have the author to put it together for us, and sadly there is not a picture, as on the puzzle box, to tell us whether we have put it together correctly. Because there is no author to consult, the surface is all we have. And yes, the Bible was actually authored—it is a human construction—whatever the source of that construction might have been. And so, because there is no author to consult, because the Bible is partial, and not transparent, you must open it up. It is a document that *must be* interpreted and you are an agent in that interpretive process.

BIBLE LITERACY CLASS: READING FOR RECALL

In recent years, a number of scholars have forcefully advocated teaching the Bible on the grounds that American students do not know basic facts about the Bible. They call this ignorance "biblical illiteracy"—a term that mirrors the work of E. D. Hirsch on cultural literacy, and misleadingly evokes the serious problems of persons who are unable to decode a written language. A more accurate descriptor is "ignorance," not "illiteracy."

The difference is significant. We all live with certain information gaps and can still flourish reasonably well. We could continue to flourish even though we might not be able to name one player of the Chicago Bears football team—

although perhaps we would not flourish in Mother's Bar on Division Street. We are much less likely to flourish if we could not decode words on a page. Advocates of biblical literacy following Hirsch have a minimum educational aim—that is, that students identify and recall biblical names and events.[2]

The two different views about reading—recall on the one side and knowing and meaning construction on the other—give rise to two different conceptions of the aims of teaching religion, which we illustrate shortly with the story of God's command to Abraham to sacrifice his son, Isaac.

The story is well-known, perhaps the most famous story in the Bible, and easily recited in a few minutes. We will address this narrative in its entirety, so it will be useful to present it here as a whole, perhaps as students in a classroom might hear (or read) it.

> After these things God tested Abraham. He said to him, "Abraham!" And he said, "Here I am." He said, "Take your son, your only son Isaac, whom you love, and go to the land of Moriah, and offer him there as a burnt offering on one of the mountains that I will show you." So Abraham rose early in the morning, saddled his donkey, and took two of his young men with him, and his son Isaac; he cut the wood for the burnt offering, and set out and went to the place in the distance that God had shown him. On the third day Abraham looked up and saw the place far away. Then Abraham said to his young men, "Stay here with the donkey; the boy and I will go over there; we will worship, and then we will come back to you." Abraham took the wood of the burnt offering and laid it on his son Isaac, and he himself carried the fire and the knife. So the two of them walked on together. Isaac said to his father Abraham, "Father!" And he said, "Here I am, my son." He said, "The fire and the wood are here, but where is the lamb for a burnt offering?" Abraham said, "God himself will provide the lamb for a burnt offering, my son." So the two of them walked on together. When they came to the place that God had shown him, Abraham built an altar there and laid the wood in order. He bound his son Isaac, and laid him on the altar, on top of the wood. Then Abraham reached out his hand and took the knife to kill his son. But the angel of the Lord called out from heaven, and said, "Abraham, Abraham!" And he said, "Here I am." He said, "Do not lay your hand on the boy or do anything to him; for now I know that you fear God, since you have not withheld your son, your only son, from me." And Abraham looked up and saw a ram, caught in a thicket by its horns. Abraham went and took the ram and offered it up as a burnt offering instead of his son. So Abraham called that

place "The Lord will provide;" as it is said to this day, "On the mount of the Lord it shall be provided." So Abraham returned to his young men, and they arose and went together to Beer-sheba; and Abraham lived in Beer-sheba. (Genesis 22:1–19)

If recall is the primary aim of a Bible as Literature class, a student's achievement could easily be assessed by a simple multiple-choice quiz:

1. What Did God Say to Abraham? (A) Hello I am God; (B) Do What I say; (C) Go to the land of Moriah; (D) Pray every day.
2. Abraham's son was named: (A) Aaron; (B) Moses; (C) Jacob; (D) Isaac.
3. Abraham took a_____ to help carry his equipment: (A) Horse; (B) Camel; (C) Donkey; (D) Mule.
4. God told Abraham to sacrifice: (A) His Son; (B) His Horse; (C) His Camel; (D) His Money.
5. Abraham carried: (A) Rocks; (B) Gun; (C) Bow and Arrow; (D) Knife.
6. Abraham went back to: (A) Beer-sheba; (B) Jerusalem; (C) Mecca; (D) Mt. Sinai.

This brief, hypothetical quiz covers the entire span of the narrative, and indeed we have structured it similarly to the form of the "warm-up" exercises that Mr. Black daily assigned to his students and to the quizzes supplied to teachers who use the NCBCPS curriculum *The Bible in History and Literature*.[3] It also has an impeccable logic behind it. Most teachers experience some anxiety about covering *the material*, and this anxiety feeds a certain conception of good teaching that students themselves pick up. Students are expected to know their facts and to be able to recite them quickly and accurately. And the more facts, the better the course. This view of education has taken on the label "literacy." When teachers are clear about their aims and have confidence in them this anxiety may be mitigated. A humanities approach offers a different possibility.

READING FOR MEANING: DETACHMENT AND THE ART OF SLOW READING

Religion as a humanistic subject has two phases. The first is developing the perspective of an insider. Through stories, music, and poetry children become attached to a certain tradition and way of understanding their world. The attachment of the insider may be followed by another stage, detachment, or the capacity to distance oneself from the immediate and primary traditions in order to explore their meanings and possibilities. In contrast to the idea that the meaning of the Bible is objective (in the sense that it is fixed and the same for everyone, as we find in the literacy approach), a pedagogy of detachment encourages students to explore a story in detail and to discover meanings. Consequently, this approach to studying Bible as "literature" allows that meaning may change or deepen as the story is read closely. In contrast to the aim of biblical literacy, which is to transmit as much information as possible to the students, detachment requires fewer facts and a much slower reading.

Here is an example from a lesson that we conducted with Ms. Smith's Bible class. The instructor of the day is Richard Layton and the topic is the same story quoted earlier. Layton developed this lesson by adapting techniques used in college-level classrooms in Israel by Elie Holzer. Holzer's primary model is a "pedagogy of the text," in which the teacher allows the text to do pedagogical work by establishing a context that promotes a transformative encounter with the reader.[4] The main ingredients of this encounter are a collaborative environment and encouraging the students to read a text at a very slow and deliberate pace. Layton applied this approach to the story of the *akedah*, the "Binding of Isaac" by his father Abraham in Genesis 22, first in his own college classrooms and then, as an experiment, in Donna Smith's Lakeside Bible class.

The class lasted for ninety minutes, and Layton began by contrasting two different forms of reading—the first he called reading in "real time" and provided examples such as road signs, instructions for constructing a cabinet, and a user's manual for electronic equipment. The essential feature that unites all these examples is that the act of reading is goal oriented; once you have the necessary information, then the reading stops. When the goal of reading is to extract the relevant information, then reading should be accomplished as quickly as possible—in such reading the text is consumed, rather than meditatively chewed. Layton then invited the students to think of reading differently—as a journey where the journey is a part of the meaning of the text, where the object is not to just reach the destination but also to enjoy the process, and where a part of that process is the change that occur in one's own understanding through meaning making. Students were told that this kind of reading is slow, careful, and collaborative: questions are asked, the experience of others is invited and answers are shared.

Then the students were told that they would read the story of the sacrifice of Abraham, with which most were familiar, but that they would read it only one sentence at a time. The sentence would be projected onto a screen and then they would be asked in groups to reflect on each sentence with the following questions in mind.

- What is the most important word or phrase in the sentence?
- How does this sentence change what I saw before?
- How does it affect what I expect will happen next?
- Discuss the sentence.

Layton emphasized that there were no right or wrong answers. Then he projected the story on to the board, one verse at a time: Here is the first line of the story again—read slowly.

After these things God tested Abraham. He said to him, "Abraham!" And he said, "Here I am."

The students, now placed in groups, were asked to deliberate among themselves and respond in writing to the following:

- I think the main thing this story will be about is:
- The most important word or phrase in the sentence is:
- The main question I have at this point in the story is:

Then another brief portion was projected on the board and the exercise continued until the story was over. After each verse the students were asked to respond to the following:

- My view of the character of Abraham at this point in the story can be best described as:_____
- The most important word or phrase to this point in shaping this view of Abraham is:_____
- I expect that next Abraham will:_____

At the outset, students responded strongly to the cues provided by God's command and Abraham's response. They characterized Abraham as the hero of the

TOURO COLLEGE LIBRARY

story, exhibiting qualities such as faithfulness, trust, obedience, loyalty, and determination. The most important word for all the groups was "test," which appears at the very outset of the story, and initially controlled how the students responded to the narrative. At this point, the students were reading the story through a traditional lens and focusing largely on the relationship between Abraham and God. The traditional reading is simple—God tested Abraham; Abraham obeyed God and passed the test, and thus he appropriately received God's praise and reward.

As the individual sentences gradually superceded each other, however, the students began to detach their focus from the relationship between Abraham and God and turn it toward the relationship between Abraham and Isaac. The turning point varied from student to student, but the guiding cue for all of Ms. Smith's students was found in the dialogue between Abraham and other characters in the story. They began to notice that Abraham's words could bear alternative meanings. For instance, when he says to the young men, "Stay here with the donkey; the boy and I will go over there; we will worship, and then we will come back to you," is he telling them what he believes to be true? If so, does he ever intend to complete the commanded sacrifice? If not, is Abraham lying? Students at this point began to experiment with other qualities that might be applied to Abraham, such as "deceitful," and "manipulative," that complicated the monochromatic portrait they initially drew of the patriarch. It was as if the students suddenly realized that Isaac is not informed of the reason for the journey and was not a participant in the decision to make it. Hence, Abraham's virtue as a devoted believer and obedient servant to God changes as he could also be seen as a parent leading his son on.

The primary goal of the lesson was to have students understand themselves as interpreters of the text, and to see that there can be internal differences and tensions in the way a text can be understood by the same reader, or in a group of readers. The students did, in fact, articulate the ambiguity of the *akedah* narrative. At the same time, they did not fully recognize the significance of their own interpretive agency. In the post-exercise survey (after Layton left the room), they told us they enjoyed the exercise, but that they did not want to have to read that slowly because it would take them forever to get through all of the material they needed to cover. Clearly the students were well socialized to conceiving reading as an instrumental, rather than reflective, practice! That is, it was our conclusion that the students were able to exhibit strong interpretive skills when provided sufficient cues, but they were less prepared to recognize themselves as *interpreters*, and consequently, did not place value on the moment of self-recognition. We concluded that if such an exercise were to be incorporated as a part of high-school syllabi, it would also be necessary for the teacher to mirror back to the students how they had actually shifted their interpretive focus and their character assessment in the process, and to draw out the implications.

The object is not to require that students change belief or to undermine those who believe that the Bible has one correct meaning. The object is to provide students with the basic understanding that would be required to make an interpretive shift should students choose to take it. There are other ways the class might go. Students could probe the relationship between trust and obedience, as they understand it; the teacher could show them how different religious figures and commentators have understood the passage, and so on. Here, the Abraham story disciplines the discussion, and as the students' insights develop they would bracket their own religious understanding and make their own preunderstanding and subsequent responses part of the analysis. Detachment—the term we give to this kind of bracketing of belief—does not require a change in the content of belief, but it does ask for a change in the way belief is held. It brings into focus the interpretive moments in a text without insisting that one turn or the other is necessarily correct. To cultivate the disposition of detachment does insist, however, on going beyond simple recognition into interpretive complexity, which teaches students not to abandon belief, but to engage it in a more systematic and reflective way.

This exercise illustrates the potential *educational* value of a Bible course that would enable students to probe their own habits of reading and to become aware of the understandings that they bring to a text. To put it in other words, the Bible as Literature course can help students bring to the surface their "preunderstandings" of the biblical text and make these implicit assumptions available for their own reflection. We stress the word "educational" to mark the distinguishing features of a Bible course taught to make students mindful of their own habits of reading and thinking from ones that stress other goals—school/community harmony, or character development, for example. These are not, of course, mutually exclusive goals. In fact, reading mindfully and with concern for one's own bias, is, as we will see in the next chapter, an important trait of character. In the remainder of this chapter we want to discuss the kinds of traits that are required for mindfulness of this kind, and how a Bible as Literature course can, if properly taught, help to develop them.

INTERPRETATION, DETACHMENT, AND
JUDGMENT: ELEMENTS OF A LIBERAL EDUCATION

Bible as Literature and world-religion courses, which we look at in the next chapter, have a unique potential to develop reflective critical thinking and discursive skills. They provide an opportunity for students to distance themselves from their own prized beliefs, to gain perspective on them, and to see new interpretive possibilities. These skills are a critical component of judgment, and hence of a moral education.

As Bekoff and Pierce note in their book on animal morality: morality requires more than emotion. It requires the capacity to assess situations that do not affect you personally. "You need a kind of distance. You need to be able to play the role of what philosophers call the 'impartial spectator' and make moral judgments about situations that don't directly affect you."[5] The phrase "play a role" needs to be emphasized. To play a role does not require that you give up yourself to the other or that you abandon your own interests and commitments. It requires that you gain perspective on them, and work to see them in the contexts of the interests and commitments of others. Moral judgment also requires the capacity to gain distance on situations that do affect you, and, in turn, moral education requires the development of an internal generalizing perspective—one that can reflect on one's own immediate desires and self-interested judgments and to reconstruct them when warranted. The ability to do this is what we call "detachment."

Detachment is the capacity to reflect on one's own self-interested judgments and the preunderstandings and beliefs that support them. By preunderstanding, we mean those beliefs that largely exist below the surface—unacknowledged—and, if they go unchallenged, will remain unchanged. For example in the 1960s and '70s, because the vast majority of physicians were white men, most people assumed that only white men were smart enough to be physicians. Thus, in any hospital, if two people—one a white man and the other a black woman—came out to look at a patient, the assumption, almost always correct, was often that the man was the doctor and the woman the nurse. If anyone noticed and asked why this was the case, there were many reasons—from "women must raise families" to "they don't have the scientific intelligence required"—to justify the arrangement. These reasons, activated only when called upon but serving always to guide judgment and determine norms, we call "preunderstandings."

Bible courses have a unique potential to bring many of these preunderstandings to the surface because, as Nel Noddings argues, students are engaged by religious concerns and are seeking answers.[6] This engagement is an aspect of adolescence that schools often ignore but that could be used to enable student's preunderstandings to be held up as a mirror and to initiate disciplined inquiry. To take an example from an earlier chapter, Mr. Milsap's mistake was not just to use his student's question about God's punishment to proselytize, but rather to cut off inquiry by supplying an immediate response to the student's bafflement. The practical question is not whether students could truly appreciate and benefit from a course that promoted intellectual dispositions, but how to do so in a way that respects both their own individual beliefs and the values of the local community.

DISPOSITIONAL SKILLS AND THE LIMITS OF EDUCATIONAL LEGITIMACY

Detachment is not usually advanced as a goal of Bible teaching. Resistance to it as an educational aim comes because of its association with a cool distancing and an inability to form commitments. Yet this is the mark of alienation, not of detachment. Alienation involves estrangement from a part of one's self, from critical features of one's identity. Detachment, on the other hand, involves holding out a part of oneself for inspection as a way, not to get rid of it, but to refine or develop it, and is a critical disposition for self-inquiry and hence for growth. To return to the aforementioned example about gender in medical fields, when the patient is first confronted with the news that the doctor is the woman and the nurse is the man, detachment allows that to be registered as surprise, rather than as a violation of sanctified norms. This moment of self-distancing serves as an occasion to bring to the surface for examination the beliefs that comprised the person's preunderstandings: one engages the fact of one's surprise and tries to understand its source. In contrast to alienation from self and identity, detachment assumes a continuing attachment. In our example, the now enlightened patient recognizes that the proper commitment is not to gendered roles but to the healing process and the institutions that best further it.

Attachment, detachment, and commitment are all aspects of a humanistic education. A person practices detachment in order to understand what is a worthwhile commitment. In the process, the person becomes conscious of previously unconscious engagements and develops capacity consciously to choose new attachments or to confirm prior ones. Detachment is required to promote self-inquiry and to evaluate immediate concerns, ambitions, and desires. It facilitates a movement toward self-renewal. Detachment, as we are using the term, is a temporary, but continuing, process of suspending belief, commitment, and desire for the sake of greater understanding, enlarged perspective, and refined commitment and desire. It does not mean abandoning belief and commitment, or resisting emotional connection. Detachment is not cold aloofness, lack of caring, or indifference; it is, rather, a stepping back from habitualized practices, meanings, and motivation in order to see them from a different, more complex perspective.

Detachment from habitual belief is the capacity that Mr. Watson sought in himself when he insisted that his course not become a testimonial for Jesus and when he found himself reassessing the presentation of the prison ministry for doing just that. He was able to step back from the formative factors that shaped him in order to help his students explore them in a larger context of meaning. His discomfort with the Lord's Harvest presentation was not (to our knowledge at least) a disagreement with their substantive positions, but rather with the inability to create the space for reflection in the classroom. His was not a ceasing to believe, but a bracketing of belief in order to meet his professional commitment not to allow his students to be indoctrinated.

Detachment is a discipline requiring complex skills of interpretation and critical analysis. Again, a Bible course has the potential to teach students some of these skills, such as temporarily bracketing belief for the sake of more informed understanding and commitment. Whether or not students can recite chapter and verse, the Bible matters, and because it does matter a Bible course has considerable potential for helping students explore their own commitment and belief in a critical and sensitive way.

There is a stage of religious development where beliefs, practices, and commitments are shaped unconsciously. Some people remain at this level throughout their lives, and this un-self-conscious practice can serve a purpose by reinforcing the coherence and solidarity of a community. A person's absence at church is noticed and members of the congregation express concern for the person's well-being. To say with slightly raised voice "I noticed you weren't in church last week, were you ill?" is to express concern about an individual and also to express unease about a potential for lost solidarity. For a Jew to ask on Yom Kippur, "are you fasting today?" can be also taken as: are you still an observant Jew? Some devout believers fear detachment because they fear it leads to exit. Sometimes it does. Yet this need not be the case, as detachment may also enrich a received commitment. Moreover, detachment from one's primary religious community is critical for public formation in religiously pluralistic societies. Where religious boundaries are made more rigid, strangers will have little opportunity to consciously shape a common fate.

How might a Bible as Literature course contribute to this disposition? Analysis, or the ability to disassemble a narrative into its component parts, is an important component of detachment. It is analogous to taking apart an engine to see how it works (or doesn't work). Moreover, detachment entails critical skills to recognize and assess different points of view, which in turn promotes self-understanding—a moment when one realizes not only "I hold this position," but that "I hold this position because of X." That "because of X" may produce a more firmly held commitment, but it implicitly recognizes that another person might come to a different conclusion "because of Y."

Literature is a field where the suspension of belief and the bracketing of commitment is an integral part of the discipline of reading a text, and Bible as Literature courses provide opportunities for students to become conscious of their own belief formation and the belief formation of others in a structured and disciplined way. For many students, the Bible is like few other texts. Students are invested in it whether they are religious or not. To frame the Bible as "literature" is neither to label it fiction or fact, but to open it to inspection through certain established categories—character development, plot, style of presentation, meaning(s), and the like. A story need not be classified as true or false to be analyzed as literature. The categories of literature are tools that can be used in different ways. Yet once one is in possession of those tools they can be applied to different kinds of texts. While Bible as Literature courses can develop a capacity for detachment, they have limited ability to provide an understanding of the religious beliefs and practices of others. This would require a familiarity with the ways in which others give meaning to their world. In the next chapter, we explore how this familiarity is developed in world religion classes and the role it can serve in constructing a civic good.

Chapter 7

WORLD RELIGIONS
Reflection as an Educational Goal

World-religion courses have two important roles to play in the shaping of a civic public. First, they can provide accurate information about different religions, correcting misinformation and stereotypes. Second, they can prepare future citizens for engagement as members of a multireligious liberal democracy. Many Americans are quite ignorant about other religions. As Diane Moore notes, "because the two primary sources of information about religion are the media and people's own faith traditions (or none), relatively few people possess even a basic understanding of the tenets of the world's religious traditions, let alone an understanding of the complex ways that religion influences and is influenced by social, cultural, and historical forces."[1] Some of this misinformation is harmless, even humorous. One of us has met friendly neighbors who grew up in east central Illinois, who admitted they were raised with the belief that Jews had horns, and who recalled when meeting her first Jew as a child glancing inconspicuously at his head to try and see the stubs. Some misinformation is more dangerous, such as the belief that Muslims are terrorists. Misinformation, ignorance, and stereotypes are serious problems for multireligious liberal societies where civic life requires a reasonable level of trust across religious differences. Addressing misinformation about other people and groups is a critical role of public education, and given the systematic misunderstanding of different religions, a systematic approach to the study of religion is needed.

The philosopher John Rawls notes many of the ideals of political liberalism rest on a consensus drawn from different religious and philosophical comprehensive worldviews. In our view, this consensus is not static but continues to evolve, even as religions change. Religions are multifaceted and dynamic, adjusting to changes both within and without, and the consensus needs constant renewal—requiring mindfulness and a continued willingness to seek out accurate information where misinformation prevails. These requirements are unlikely to be met if all that students understand about other religious traditions is learned from their own tradition or from distorted media accounts. By studying world religions, students can begin to recognize the religious strangers as entwined in a shared fate and as coagents in building a common future, both of which are conditions of a liberal democracy. In this chapter, we examine schools that have a sophisticated world-religion program and we use that program to argue that the critical element of recognition is a certain form of respect, which we then analyze.

THE PROGRAM IN WORLD RELIGION: MAKING THE STRANGE FAMILIAR AND THE FAMILIAR STRANGE

While the majority of students at both Johnson High and Eastland High schools are Christian, each school also has a significant minority of students from other religious backgrounds with a representation of Muslims, Jews, and Hindus. Moreover, both schools are close to large metropolitan areas with considerable religious diversity. While Johnson High, with its 4,500 students, is located in a small town, it has five different elementary districts that feed their students into it. Eastland High, with its 2,500 students, is located in a larger bedroom community of 45,000 people. It is religiously diverse and takes pride in the fact that it is "home to many religious groups" including Muslims, Jews, Christians, Hindus, and Mormons. It is a wealthy community, by far the wealthiest we visited for this study. The median household income is over $100,000 and the median home value is over half a million dollars. Over 85 percent of its population is white, with the remaining population divided among Asian (10 percent), Hispanic (4 percent), and African American (1.5 percent) residents. This is still a largely Caucasian population, but dramatically more diverse than Ridge and Jordan counties. A number of major national corporations have offices and facilities in the immediate area surrounding the township. Because the world-religion program at Eastland is the older and more robust of the two programs, and served as the model for the program at Johnson, we focus largely on its program, and draw on Johnson to exemplify a few points.

There are two public high schools in the Eastland area: Eastland High, where our study took place, and South Eastland High, where a newer offshoot program has developed. By most standards, these are very good schools. Eastland's graduation rate is over 99 percent, and the average score on both the ACT and the SAT tests in all areas is well above the national average. 98 percent of the graduates go on to higher education, many to highly rated four-year colleges. Compared to the other schools in this study, Johnson students receive a very advantaged education, with *US News and World Report* listing it as one of the best high schools in the country. The two schools have a strong international flavor, as is indicated by the presence of the International Baccalaureate program in one of them—a premier program for high-achieving students that coordinates its offerings with similar programs throughout the United States and in other countries—and by the program in world religion.

The program in world religion at Eastland was initiated by Mr. Miller, now the head of the social studies department. At the time of our study the program had been in operation for almost three decades, and grew out of his teaching the world history course in the early 1980s, in response to his students' many questions about religion. As a young teacher in 1982 he attended an intensive, five-week workshop sponsored by a national foundation called the Religious Study Project, which he describes as one of his most valuable academic experiences of his career. He began teaching a world-religions course in the fall of 1983. After eight years, the demand for the course was so great, and the time so short, that he split the course into two separate classes—one for Eastern religions; the other for Western. Now there are six sections of Eastern religions and four sections of Western religions each year.

The courses began as a program for honors students, but it is now open to all upper-class students. Presently, three people teach the courses: in addition to Mr. Miller, we had the chance to observe and interview two more junior, but still highly experienced colleagues, Mr. Bradley and Ms. Freeman. Western religion covers Judaism, Christianity, and Islam, while Eastern covers Buddhism, Hinduism, and Chinese religion. Miller tells us that the goals of the course have remained essentially the same over the years and lists them as follows:

1. To ask what is religion—discuss/define the concept
2. To appreciate diversity—both commonalities among religions and differences between religions
3. To analyze why religious people construct their worlds through religion (using symbols, myths, ritual practices, etc.)
4. To become aware of the need for dialogue in society (especially since September 11)
5. To make the familiar strange and the strange familiar
6. To gain academic and critical skills

Each class takes two field trips a term to places of worship, usually in the nearby metropolitan area, during a time when services are conducted. The honors students complete a project in which they must also attend a religious service by themselves and interview a religious leader. As mentioned earlier, Miller's influence has now spread beyond Eastland to the other high school in the town, as well as to Johnson High School. Both of these now have versions of world-religion courses, although they are packaged as studies of both Eastern and Western traditions in the same course.

In contrast to Tearville and Ridge, where the teachers assume a coherent, religious local community and strive to reproduce it through the Bible classes, the teachers at Eastland and Johnson are aware of the absence of a well-defined, single coherent religious community—an absence that is reflected in the religious diversity of their school. Where the wall between school and church was exceptionally porous at Tearville and Ridge, teachers at both Johnson and Eastland have a strong sense of the boundary between school and religion. In cases where students are attracted to a religion as a result of studying it in school, as sometimes does happen, the teachers encourage the student to inform his or her parents. Local religious leaders and congregations are seen as resources for the students to draw on, but outside speakers, while welcomed, are carefully briefed, and religious literature is scrutinized, hence avoiding the kind of situation that occurred with the prison ministry at Jordan High.

Because of high levels of physical and economic mobility, teachers see themselves as preparing their students for a life beyond Eastland and Johnson and for a world of religious diversity. The world-religion courses are intended to simulate those unknown future, multireligious communities, and teachers speak of training global citizens and world leaders. They do not present themselves to their students as experts on every aspect of religion and view the religious diversity of student body and the general population as important resources in developing global citizens. To whatever extent possible they try to find ways to represent the religion in an "authentic" way, which in their minds means to provide the point of view of an ideal practitioner: devout, knowledgeable, and supportive of his or her religious tradition. Teachers at times rely on their students to inform them and other students about their beliefs and practices. For example, in a segment on Islam, the teacher invited members of the Muslim Student club to give a presentation and answer questions submitted by their fellow students, which ranged from the fasting requirement of Ramadan to parental supervision of dating.

The courses are expected to be academically rigorous—an expectation which, given the lack of published material designed for high-school students, presents a challenge for the teachers. To meet this challenge, teachers have developed their own materials from many different sources. They have also used college-level texts such as Huston Smith's *The World's Religions*, which many of their students find quite difficult. They may also assign books like Harold Kushner's *To Life: A Celebration of Jewish Being and Thinking*, to help students better understand a particular religion and its people. Although the courses are academically rigorous, teachers also view them as an opportunity to interrupt the daily grind of striving after grades and competing to be number one in a very high-achieving school. As a result, motivation is not an issue and failure is very unusual. As one teacher describes it:

> Well first of all, almost all students do well in this class and we to this day don't know why. We have very few kids who fail; we have very few Ds. A student in U.S. History right now who has a social worker involved, all these [professional] people involved [in helping her][2] she flourished in that class. We give them very difficult material; we expect them to write a lot, things that ordinarily will knock out about 10 percent of your group. They for whatever reason, I think part of it is they chose to be there, I think part of it is the depth that we go in. We don't rush through things so I think we end up getting everybody by the time we get to the end point. Our class is an oasis for some types of kids. We do a lot of artwork; we listen to a lot of music, so there is certainly going to be a type of kid who in that environment would thrive.

The courses help some students navigate their own spiritual quest by exploring the beliefs and practices of other religions. It is here where some of the most knotty problems can arise for these teachers: how to respond to the student who tells them he or she wants to convert, or to one student who told the teacher that she believes that she might be a bodhisattva, born to bring enlightenment to others. When confronted with personal spiritual issues the teachers try to refer the student to their parents for guidance, hence respecting parental authority by affirming a division of labor between the personal and the academic, the family and the school.

At the end of the day, however, the teachers want the students to become agents in their own education about religion and to be able to claim their own beliefs in an intelligent way. What this boils down to in practice is that the teachers work to help the students map out, both internally as well as externally, the field of religious beliefs, and to be able thereby to locate their own beliefs within that field.

The need to address growing national and global diversity, to foster relations between students with different religious backgrounds, were recurring themes in our discussions with the teachers, as was the need to help students to own their religious identity. These classes provide opportunities for the students at Eastland and Johnson to display their religious commitments—in dress or through membership—in school religious clubs. In this way, they are not dissimilar from Tearville or Ridge, where students often wore the name of their religious camp or church on their shirts or jackets. The difference is simply in the diversity itself and in the teacher's reliance on students from different traditions to serve as informants.

The course promotes reflection and detachment. To quote Mr. Miller, the course aims to "make the familiar strange and the strange familiar." At times, making the familiar strange involves basic religious literacy. Students not only learn about the Nicene Creed and its centrality to the Christian faith for example; they also learn about the political motives of Constantine in convening a council to determine the status of the Son within the Godhead.

Making the familiar strange also can entail presenting the beliefs of a familiar religion, usually Christianity, from the standpoint of a less familiar one. So in addition to learning about the Trinity and trying to make sense of it from a Christian standpoint, students are also informed that many Muslims and some Jews see Christianity as a polytheistic religion and view the doctrine of the Trinity as promoting the worship of three gods. Students learn about the diversity *between* different religions, *and also* about the diversity *within* different religions, their own included. The strange is made familiar through field trips, interviews with religious leaders and invited speakers, and of course through lectures, art, and music. Teachers encourage students to seek out and listen to firsthand accounts of different religion by congregants and religious leaders themselves. And, perhaps most important, they teach students how to display respect while engaged in serious discussions about religion.

The teachers view the course as special and devote a great deal of time and emotional energy to it. As Ms. Freeman describes it:

> Sometimes it's about being in the zone that day. Sometimes I wake up in the morning and have a concept to teach and I go, "I'm not feeling it, I'm not feeling like I'm in the zone today and I have to be on." Never do I have to feel that way in a U.S. History class, I can just turn it on. There is just an automatic switch, but how to teach other things in an Eastern World Religions class I have to channel something. I don't know what it is but it's exciting and fun and I think the conversations in World Religions about human nature from these various points of views, about ethical conduct from various points of view, is so meaningful and that's important to me that they have that deep meaning and they have that deep understanding.

Mr. Bradley describes the difference between teaching world religions and world history:

> I have world history class and I have world religions. World religions classes take up 80 percent of my life here because I have to walk in well prepared in my religions classes. I have to be on top of my game. Because students will ask questions that I just have to be ready for all the time.
>
> As much as I present it as an academic subject, for me it's emotional. And it is psychological and it is spiritual. I have to separate myself from my role as an academic when I walk into that classroom. That takes some time. That takes discipline and it takes a lot of self-examination and I think that that's emotionally draining at times. And it's wonderful.
>
> The kids come in with their baggage. They're all coming in with their different views on religion, different levels of devotion, different levels of faith, dif-

ferent levels of frustration with religion, and everybody comes into this room together. And somehow you've got to present the information in a way that is somewhat academic. Even though you know that all this other stuff is going on. Even though you know that there are kids that are going home to environments where their parents are frustrated with them or not pleased with them at the level of their devotion. Or maybe they're devout and their parents aren't. A lot goes on.

Religion is a highly charged subject to teach in the academic environment. These teachers welcome the challenge of the material, but most of all they welcome the religious diversity of the students and often use it to engage them actively in their own education. The enthusiasm is visible in the work that the teachers put into the course, in the number of workshops they have attended, in the courses they have enrolled in over the years, the study trips they have taken, and in the preparation time they take in locating and reproducing material for the course.

RESPECT AS EMPATHY: THE AESTHETIC MODE

One way that teachers at Eastland promote respect is by providing students with an aesthetic appreciation of religion. By "aesthetic," we mean an understanding that touches the students emotionally as an art object might. The goal is to go beyond simple literacy and provide the students with a point of contact with the motivating power of the religion. When this happens, the material takes on an aesthetic dimension, where the students begin to understand how a spiritual tradition helps people address the concerns of everyday life. Students then gain an appreciation of the role a religion plays in the various aspects of a life. Mr. Miller glosses this goal as "making the strange familiar," but the strange can be made familiar in different ways. Ms. Freeman explains how she works to bring students into emotional connection with the religion by exposing them to a basic human experience, like suffering.

> When I walk into my U.S. History class and when I walk into my Eastern Religions class, I sort of chuckle to myself about the magnitude of the difference in terms of the subtleties of what needs to be taught. The First Noble Truth in Buddhism is that life is suffering. OK, we can cover that in a minute [in history]

and they can write that down in their notebook and we can move on. In World Religions I can really spend a couple days having them probe that and deeply think about what the suffering in their lives and in the world and what the Buddha meant by that. In a typical history class, there's not that subtlety of trying to teach something that is so immense and so often so beyond words that it presents a different type of challenge and I think it's one we take on. I think we could take the easy way out and fly through some of this stuff and they could have a very kind of a surface understanding, but we choose to go deeper and make this more philosophical and something they know on a deeper level and therefore it's a very challenging thing to do as a teacher when you're talking to 15 and 16 year olds. Going back to the life of suffering, we often have two groups of people in the room. One whose lives have been very difficult and they know that. But the other group, who you know la-la-la-la-la is, "Life is suffering? Really?" have no clue. And then trying to show both of those sides and the subtle ways in which the Buddha thought we suffered like we want to flip someone off at the red light and how that all works and how that all manifests. It takes time to do that and it takes a skill that's much different than presenting something that is in a straightforward history class. Here, if we really want them to understand Buddhism it's not necessarily enough to stop at that surface understanding and we're looking for a deep understanding of these traditions. That requires going into territories that require a great skill to teach.

Life is suffering, that sounds so compact but that idea is much bigger than that statement. And so we're going for a deeper understanding. And that's what I think distinguishes this class from a World History class where you're getting just a quick contextual understanding of a philosophy in a unit on India or Taoism in a unit on China.

By a "deeper understanding," Ms. Freeman means an emotional engagement with the meaning of suffering and of the religious traditions that address it in particular. Hence, her classes include a lot of artwork that is intended to help the students understand the worldview of the religion under discussion and the way it connects to the human project. When she is successful in helping students understand the way in which a tradition like Buddhism speaks to suffering and to the everyday trials of everyday human existence, she has helped, in the words of Mr. Miller, to make the strange familiar. Familiarity is achieved not by reducing the "strange" religion to the ideas of a familiar one, but rather by reaching into the common experiences of humanity—birth, death, suffering, our connections to one another and to nature—and then by showing how a specific religion provides helps to shape the meaning of these experiences. The message is not that all religions are the same, but that all religious people must come to terms with similar aspects of the human experience. Granted, this is not always easy for some high-school students to grasp, but the course can be valuable for them at other levels as well. It can bring students to understand that there is a deeper level of experience and thought, even if they may not yet be ready to engage fully with the ideas. Ms. Freeman explains the way the course is appropriated by students at different levels.

> I definitely think there are kids who take this course that don't walk out at the end of the semester with the depth I'm looking for because they're not capable, they're not ready, but they're having fun and sometimes I think they think they're kind of cool because they're in a class where these intelligent conversations are going on. But I would say the great majority of our kids were kind of attracted to this class because they had that kind of thinking, they were philosophical, they can think abstractly. These are kids who think deeply about life.

This remark contrasts sharply with Mr. White in Tearville who was convinced that his students simply wanted to stay on the surface and did not want to probe deeply. Ms. Freeman allows that there are some students who are not yet ready to probe beyond the surface, but in emphasizing the connection between religions and the universal elements of human experience she provides the ground for recognition of the other and respect for their beliefs and practices.

Beyond this basic level of information transfer, students are taught to view a religion as they might a painting—as a coherent meaningful object, an object that they need to try to understand before they can judge. At the aesthetic level, for example, a teacher gives a lecture on Taoist art and then students are given a homework assignment to develop an art form that reflects the Taoist mode and displays an understanding of the Taoist tradition. Students later are asked to explain their work in class and how it reflects a Taoist perspective. The object is not to make the students good artists in the Taoist tradition, but to make them aware of their own taken for granted categories of cognition and judgment, what the teachers label ethnocentrism. Ms. Freeman tells us that she seeks to cultivate respect from the very outset of the course.

We spend a lot of time—two weeks in the beginning of the unit—trying to go with them through a series of lessons, what it means to be open-minded, to be as nonjudgmental as possible. We always tell them that it's probably impossible to be completely free of judgment, but to be aware of it and to really try to learn about these religions as right for other people and to move forward with that. And the idea that something that is right for you can often interfere in your ability to understand or even respect something that's right for someone that challenges what is right for you. So that idea of respect starts with an understanding and awareness that something can be right for you and something different can be right for someone else. And to just kind of leave it at that: it's not what would work for you, that's not how you see it or how you would do it, but they do. And it doesn't have to be a contest, no one has to win, it's just that people have different ideas and to respect that.

DETACHMENT

Detachment, as we saw in the last chapter, involves a temporary disengagement from one's own taken-for-granted framework. With Ms. Smith, we saw how detachment can be used to refine interpretation. It can also be used to refine judgment. To this end, the teachers in the world-religion courses work to make students aware of their own preunderstandings and to help them develop ways to discipline them. Much of this involves simply bringing students to the awareness that their cognition and judgment are influenced by and reflect what we call their uncritical preunderstanding. Teachers spend a considerable amount of time helping students to recognize their own patterns of cognition and judgment. Sometimes this involves opening up students to the religious differences that exist among them—as for example, when members of the Muslim students group were invited to present and answer questions about Islam—but at other times it involves the simple awareness that they *do* in fact have their own preunderstandings and that these influence judgment. The following is an example of an exercise given at the beginning of a class on Eastern religions.

> I give them three questions that they're going to answer about each of the people whose photograph I project on a screen and ask: what is your first impression of this person? Does this person remind you of anyone? And how does this person

make you feel? So the first photograph is a Native American woman, second photograph is an elderly white male, and the third photograph is a young black male. And so they go through this process of looking at them and judging them based on how they look and the limited knowledge they have and then we go over what they thought. They're usually completely wrong. Their assumptions are usually completely wrong because I tell them who these people actually are. The Native American woman they think is homeless and poverty stricken. The white man they think is very grandfatherly and kind and that's the person they usually choose to meet. And then, the third person they think is kind of from an African tribe. And it turns out that the Native American woman is a scholar, the white man is a white supremacist, and the black man is a Harvard-graduated stockbroker.

The students then discuss their own preunderstanding and the way it influences judgment. The aim is to teach students to defer judgment about the worth of different religions and to encourage them to explore the religion on its own terms. It is detachment not for the sake of changing belief, but for the sake of enabling students to know what they believe and how their beliefs affect judgment. When successful, it provides students with an internal monitor that interrupts hastily formed judgments about the religious other.

REFLECTION

Reflection involves developing the ability to see one's own understandings and dispositions, as reflected in the practices of one's own group, from the standpoint of others. Teachers in world-religion courses have an invaluable tool in this respect—the understandings and misunderstandings about other religions that students already hold. Ms. Williams, at Johnson High, provides an example of the way she develops reflective skills by encouraging students to see their own society from the standpoint of others. One of her favorite techniques is to engage her students in a critical discussion of an unfamiliar religion. So, for example, in her class on Hinduism she asks: "Does the caste system really divide people? Is it unfair or inequitable?" She plays devil's advocate, pointing out the Indian government laws that forbid castes, and exposes them to the argument that the United States has more of a caste system. Students then engage this

argument with examples about the cycle of poverty and the low odds of someone getting out of an impoverished social class. Hence, through a discussion of
Hinduism and the student's negative response to the idea of caste, she promotes
a discussion of poverty and immobility here in the United States. For this group
of largely privileged students, a discussion of Hinduism provides an opportunity to engage practices of their own society, not just for information sake, but
to also gain perspective and to see from another standpoint.

TRANSFORMATION

Teachers in world-religion courses hope their work is transformative—they
want students to be more reflective about their own beliefs and more open
about those of others. Yet they are aware of the fine line between transformation and indoctrination—where the one seeks to open, and the other seeks to
close the mind. They try to set the stage for transformation and quietly ap-
plaud it when it happens, but this is not an explicit aim of the course. They
may hope for change, but their respect for their students' beliefs requires that
they can only aim at changing and evaluating outward behavior. Hence, the
aims Mr. Miller lists are all academic. "To make the strange familiar" means to
learn more about other religions and to understand and appreciate their appeal. "To make the familiar strange" means to learn more about one's own—it
does not mean that one must grow to like the one better or the other worse.
Transformation depends on how the student decides to use the knowledge for
self-development. And, unlike Mr. Milsap, who had preprogrammed the end
of the desired transformation—accepting Jesus as one's personal savior—here
the end cannot be preprogrammed. For what it means to be transformed in an
open, reflective way means that the student must decide on the aim of his or her
own transformation. Yet transformations do occur, sometimes as a direct result
of the assignments.

For example, one assignment requires students to explore an unfamiliar religious community and write an essay on what they find. Students are required to
interview a leader of that community and attend a service. They must describe
the history of the community and summarize its main beliefs and practices as
understood from the readings, the observations, and the interviews. In addition,
they are also expected to dress appropriately and to be respectful and to honor

the requirements of the religion. Thus, for example, if a male student were to enter a synagogue, he would be expected to wear a yarmulke. The assignment does not ask the student to engage his or her own beliefs with those of the selected community, nor does it ask that the student write about any personal changes that took place as a result of the assignment. In other words, the assignment is for academic purposes and is evaluated in those terms. For students who do want to probe more deeply the essay allows them to do that, and thus offers transformational opportunities, as it did with this student who wrote about Jehovah's Witnesses.

> The first time I heard of Jehovah's Witnesses was on the *David Letterman* show. He was making fun of them and how they "attack" people with their beliefs. I started to make fun of them and their "crazy" ways. Then I realized what a horrible thing I was doing so I wanted the opportunity to find out more about them, and I have! When I told my family I was doing this project, they started making fun of me and saying how I was going to be brainwashed when I went to the service. I was pretty scared of going.

Except for their strong rejection of homosexuality as "ungodly and immoral," she found that she shared many of their beliefs and strongly admired their stance against war and violence. She concludes her essay:

> I really enjoyed this project. I found it to be one of the more useful things I have done in school all year. This project taught me not to judge when I know nothing about someone. This project really opened my eyes.[3]

The exercise allowed this student to detach herself from her own and her family's views about the minority Christian sect and to reflect on them such that the she can say "this project really opened my eyes," meaning that it helped her reconsider her own judgment and to understand how it was formed—through Letterman and family—and that it can be mistaken.

This is detachment not in some grand metaphysical sense—no strikes of lightning here, no road to Damascus revelation—but in the sense that allows this student to engage with people whom she had considered strange. It is the kind of modest transformation that occurs when a person comes to understand that his or her own beliefs are in part contingent on the process of his or her formation and is then alert to the possibility of holding other beliefs. This is part of what we mean when we say that the object of detachment is not belief, but believing. It is a way of being open to the role that belief serves both in one's own understanding and identity formation and the similar role that it serves in other people. Transformation need not mean changing one's own beliefs, but it does mean being alert to the possibility that change in some beliefs (as yet unknown) may at some point be warranted.

Ms. Williams' goal is not just to transmit information or to encourage self-reflection, although that is certainly a part of it, but to develop citizens who will engage with others on many different levels. Information, detachment, aesthetic appreciation, and reflection are all part of this larger transformative process. Williams explains:

> To be a good citizen, you are responsible for knowing why and how sacred elements of religion are in different parts of the world. This is not just about learning about other people, but a shared responsibility. The strongest responsibility now that they have taken the class, and they hear a slander—e.g., Muslim—it is their responsibility to correct them.

She knows this can be difficult and tells us that she has now come to feel comfortable correcting people about misconceptions and she would like her students to do the same. She counts as one of her successes a student who reported that he corrected his boss when he described the Muslim call to prayer as sounding like a "wild turkey call." While not an official aim of her course, her ideal is to transmit information for transformative purposes, hoping to provide communal as well as individual enlightenment.

TRANSFORMATION V. TRANSGRESSION

How far can Ms. Williams legitimately go in advancing this hope and engaging her students in her ecumenical project? Are there limits here just as there should have been for Mr. Milsap when he was advancing his own Christian beliefs? We think that there are distinctions that need to be considered. For example, if the student were to tell Ms. Williams in front of the class about his experience with his boss and if she were to nod her approval, we think this would be appropriate. It reinforces both an important fact about Islam and it demonstrates how the information can be applied to everyday life. In praising the student for correcting a misconception, Ms. Williams would have been encouraging all of her students to look for the relevance of the course in their everyday lives. This would be starkly different from any overt assignment to "find someone who has a misconception about Islam and correct him!"

Just as a teacher of the Bible can become overly enthusiastic in advancing his beliefs, as we saw with Mr. Milsap, world-religion teachers may have difficulty at times distinguishing their personal mission from their professional one. It is at these moments when the hope for transformation may conflict with students' rights to have their own beliefs respected for their own sake. Ms. Williams wants students to believe that all religions are basically the same and designs her class so that they will highlight the similarities. In contrast to her example with Islam, which was based on accurate information, this goal to have students believe in the underlying sameness of religions requires significant distortions. If successful, this lesson would impose on students the view that their own religion stands on an equal epistemic and spiritual plane with all others—a claim that would be impossible to verify, and, ironically, implies that we can only respect those whose beliefs resemble our own. In contrast, the teachers at Eastland are careful to distinguish between the appeal of different religions on their own terms and an accurate assessment of their commonalities and differences. As Mr. Miller explains:

> My goal is for the students to read that book and go, I can really understand why someone would want to be Jewish. For each of these traditions, I want the kids to know more than the differences between religions, but [to] understand why someone would want to be a part of that religion. It's not that we're advocating that religion; we're advocating an understanding as to why someone would want to be a member of that religion and enjoy it.

The difference here between Ms. Williams and Mr. Miller is the difference between imposing a "correct" belief in order to transform students and providing a transformative *opportunity* without transgressing the boundaries of personal religious belief.

With Mr. Miller, the emphasis is on understanding the basic elements of a religion, the way they fit together, and, as we saw with Ms. Freeman, the emphasis is on helping students to understand its emotional power. It is quite possible to satisfy this understanding in a strictly academic matter. As Ms. Freeman puts it:

> I would say that maybe as teachers in a public school environment we have to be less than idealistic in terms of what the information we present is used for. So if I could get these students to at least understand these different perspectives, I'll take that. They have a good understanding of it—I'll take that, even if they use it for denouncing, even if they use it for conversion purposes. I'll take that. And I don't necessarily see any conflict there. I can tell you that it is hard sometimes. There are times when I want to say, you know that doesn't seem quite right to me.

Ms. Freeman wants to create transformational opportunity but not by distorting the facts—by proclaiming all religions are the same—or by programming students to have a positive attitude about all religions.

While the teachers work to explain the context in which beliefs make sense, to correct misconceptions, and to alert the students to the kind of preunderstanding labeled "ethnocentrism," there are times when they are forced to acknowledge their own hesitation when it comes to accepting certain practices associated with a religious and cultural heritage. For example, Ms. Freeman is forced to admit to an "ethnocentric moment" when she recalls to her present students a former class where a seventeen-year-old student from Pakistan told her she was about to enter into an arranged marriage with an older man. Here Ms. Freeman ponders the conflict between cultural practices and individual rights. In the end she tells her present students that she comes down on the side of individual rights, modeling for her students the kind of reflexivity that she hopes to develop in them.

RESPECT AND AUTONOMY

One of the justifications for teaching world religion is to open students to the value that can be found in a plurality of religions—a justification that is inspired by a certain notion of respect and democratic citizenship. If such courses are to be successful teachers need not only to teach their students respect, but they need to model it themselves without manipulating the student to form certain friendly beliefs about other religions. Doing this requires a great deal of practical knowledge and art, especially with students who believe that their own religion is the only true one and that others are inferior or false. Some of these students are not in class to learn about the value people find in other religions, as Mr. Miller would like, but rather to learn how to convert other students and to convince them that their religion is an inferior to the one, true religion. They seek strategic, not empathetic, understanding.

In these cases, the teacher has a choice: to respect the right of the student to insist on the superiority of his or her religion in class or to establish a "do not proselytize" rule in class and thereby shut off religious expression when it is used to exalt one religion over others. If the latter route is taken, the teacher has exalted one view (the value of pluralism) over another (the truth of the Christian religion). If the former course is taken, then the teacher is orienting the students to the basic object of the course—understanding a plurality of religions—without silencing the religious chauvinist. But this course runs the danger of trespassing on other students' rights and turning the class over to those who want it to become, in Mr. Watson's earlier words, a "testimonial to Jesus."

Mr. Bradley faced this dilemma when two evangelical Christian students told him at the start of the class that their goal was to learn more about non-Christian religions so that they could be more effective in their mission to convert non-Christians as well as non-evangelical-Christians, and that their target included Bradley himself. They were vocal in class about their view that only believing Christians can be saved and that everyone else is condemned to hell. Rather than take either route—establishing "the do not proselytize rule" or insisting that the students feign appreciation—he used the occasion to teach the students how to indicate respect for someone with whom you profoundly disagree. In doing so, he was also teaching them how to engage in a certain kind of discourse.

Because he does allow his evangelical students a voice in his class, things can get heated. But rather than silencing the different sides, he uses the differences to teach them important lessons about academic norms. Here is his description of the way he channels the discussion to enable the conversation to continue:

I don't think that if an evangelical Christian says that "if you don't accept Christ then you're going to hell" it is disrespectful. This is the academic environment. In the academic environment, you are allowed to come and express your views, and if somebody else's view is offensive to you, then you have a right to respond. But it has to be done in a way you understand. And if you disagree, then you say, I disagree with that concept—and I've had students say that—I disagree with that concept because for you to say to me that I'm going to hell because I don't accept your view is both irrational to me and judgmental. Done! That's where I take them! That's allowed: that's respectful. That's what the academic environment is about. That is not disrespectful. Now if somebody said, "you know that idea is crazy, I don't even understand how you can think about that idea"—and I've had students say that—I'll say "rephrase, rephrase." And we actually teach them this before we get in, rephrase, and they'll gather themselves and they'll rephrase. And that's a great exercise. We talk about emotionally charged words and words that have more neutral charge to them. I'll say stick to academic words; crazy is not an academic word because it's open to too many different interpretations. Offensive is a good academic word. Irrational is a good academic word. Vague is a good academic word. So they choose these words, we're able to have this open discussion without people getting too upset.

An "academic word" for Mr. Bradley is one that keeps discourse going and develops the students' capacities to explain their beliefs in ways that need not exalt one religion over another. Somewhat like a choir conductor who teaches a student to hear her own voice as others hear it, non-exalting discourse teaches students to engage each other while acknowledging differences. To tell people that they are going to go to hell if they do not accept Jesus Christ sounds like an attack—repent or go to hell. A response—"that's crazy"—escalates the conflict and there is little room for an authentic, honest exchange. Exaltation takes the place of respect. Moreover, a word like "crazy" has no boundaries and cannot move the conversation forward, whereas a word like "irrational" does have some boundaries. Are the premises unclear? Is the logic faulty? To call a belief irrational is to lay down a promissory note that I can show you why I cannot accept your claim. In the process, the Christian students are also encouraged to unpack their claim—for example, "you will go to hell." Mr. Bradley elaborates:

> For example if you ask an evangelical Christian to explain themselves when they say, if you don't accept Christ, you're going to hell, often they will express

themselves, not that I'm judging you, but this is my way of showing love for you. Because in *my* belief system, unless one accepts that Jesus came to erase original sin and to save all, unless you really fully accept that, you won't get to heaven. So it's not like I think you're a bad person, and they will explain it this way, it's just that, I'll always have them rephrase "based on my faith," not as this is the way it is, but "based on my faith, according to my tradition." If you come into my classroom kids will even stop themselves, they'll start to say something one way and then they'll go back and say, "Based on my view or based on our tradition, that's how you get to heaven, you accept Christ." And so they'll explain Christian evangelizing and proselytizing as an act of love, as an act of Christian love. We care about you and about your soul. And that's how we kind of unpack that. And that's easier to swallow than when they first come out and say, "if you don't accept Christ you're going to hell." And that to me is very exciting when that happens.

When he is successful, there is a very significant transformation, but its significance is not in a changed belief but in the process of believing. Students are learning to contextualize their own perspective and to acknowledge a plurality of perspectives even while holding on to their own belief. When they say, "according to my tradition," there is an implicit recognition that there are other traditions that would see it differently, and yet I don't have to change my commitments. Bradley explains the nature of the respect that students are developing.

The average evangelical student that comes into my class, they're not going to have their mind changed, that's my experience. But do they accomplish one of our goals, which is to respect other traditions? As long as they're in my classroom and their responses are in my classroom appropriately stated and their line of questioning is appropriate, I've done my job.

Uncertainty, of course, remains. As Mr. Bradley admits: "Now, there's no way of me telling whether or not they authentically respect it," but in the classroom he is teaching them a new language, and like any new language, whether or not they choose to use it once the class has finished will depend on the student. So, Mr. Bradley has taught evangelical and non-evangelical alike a certain form of communication, where one person does not exalt himself or herself over another—a mark of disrespect—and he has managed to do so without exalting his own pluralism over any religion. He has thus managed to go through the horns of the dilemma—not, no proselytizing for pluralism, but lots of rules about language and how to engage in discourse. As he says, perhaps with bit of resignation: "So the two evangelical kids can walk out of that classroom, just talking about what happened in class, but while they're in the class they have to engage in that way." Transformation is always uncertain, as respect requires it must be.

RESPECT AND THE CONSTRUCTION OF A CIVIC PUBLIC

These two students can help us clarify something quite important about the object of respect in a liberal society. Many believers hold that there is something of special value about their own religion and they do not necessarily believe the same thing about other religions. Indeed, they may have an accurate understanding of the beliefs of other religions but also believe that they are simply wrong. The core beliefs of many religions test credulity and one of the marks of a person who is religious in that particular religion is whether or not he or she is willing to not challenge, and to let be, what others view as incredible.

What does it mean then to ask students to be respectful in situations where deep down they do feel that a particular belief is "crazy"? Or that someone will go to hell because he or she does not hold a particular belief? We think that democracy has a clear and ready-made answer for this. Democracy does not require that one accept the belief of the other nor does it require that one respect the institutional religion of the other—say as a private might respect the military even if disagreeing with its mission. Democracy requires only that one respect the believers' autonomy, or their right to form beliefs, to express their beliefs and to worship with others as they please. Autonomy, however, is a tricky business for educators. As we mentioned in the introduction, it is a status that is both to be respected as a present state and to be developed as a future one. In allowing his fundamentalist students to voice their beliefs, Mr. Bradley has met both forms of respect. He has acknowledged the students' essential right to be listened to as autonomous moral beings. In teaching them how to express these views without lording it over others, he has allowed them to appreciate the autonomy of others and has provided an opportunity to develop as more reflective, autonomous selves. Whether the students will eventually take advantage of this opportunity is another question.

PROBLEMS

The task of explaining the strange or defamiliarizing the familiar presents peda-gogical and structural issues. Consider the problem of selecting and arranging material to familiarize students with the strange. In some school subjects, for example, math, the problem does not seem especially complicated: addition be-fore multiplication, subtraction before division. The teacher can then explain the latter, the strange, in terms of the former, the familiar. However, the very aim of the world-religion course, to make the familiar strange, suggests that the teacher not give priority to familiar religious ideas and place them all on the same plane, but this can be tricky.

For example, the course in comparative religions taught at Johnson High began with a section on creation myths, which included stories from many in-digenous religions, as well as from Buddhism, Hinduism, and Shinto, but con-spicuously not from Genesis. This exclusion would seem to contradict one of the implicit goals of the course: to help students see the familiar as strange and the strange as familiar. It seems to provide respect to Christian literalism but it does so by maintaining as unchallenged the comfortable and familiar under-standing of those stories as reports of real historical events. The exclusion is also significant because it raises questions about both means and ends. To us, one of the most exciting, yet largely implicit, goals of the course is to teach students, in postmodern jargon, to decenter their own identities—what we have called detachment.

This largely means that if the course is truly successful students will have developed the skill to perceive whatever truth values they give to their own reli-gious commitments and practices as contingent on a particular kind of upbring-ing. To decenter one's own identity does not mean to abandon that identity or even to see it as equal to all others. However, it does entail an ability to recognize an innate reciprocity: the beliefs and values that one student takes for granted can be viewed as "strange" or "myth" by other students. Ideally, the student would come to understand why those students hold such views about his or her own cherished beliefs. Bracketing the biblical creation accounts from all other cre-ation myths suggests that somehow they are special and not to be viewed along the same dimension as other creation stories, and that to treat them in this way preserves students' preunderstanding. It is respect by neglect.

At the same time, there is not a hard-and-fast rule. Some students may not be ready to view their own stories as akin to myths, and to hit them over the head with the idea that all creation stories are mythical may well be counterproductive to the long-range value of the course. Yet if one of the goals of the course is to enable students to be aware of their own preunderstanding—to make the familiar strange—it would be useful for students to understand that some people do accept the two quite different creation stories as historically accurate and that some view them as myths. The fact that there is no clear and ready answer to this and many other issues that the teaching of religion raises for public schools points to an important need in teacher preparation if the potential of religion courses for the improvement of civic discourse is to be accomplished.

Chapter 8

PROBLEMS, RESERVATIONS, AND RECOMMENDATIONS

Religion courses can add considerably to a student's general fund of knowledge. They can provide insights into intellectual and cultural foundations of modern societies. They can balance the utilitarian aims of much of the modern curriculum. They can provide students with ample material for critical thinking and self-reflection, as well as with opportunities to encounter the religious "other" in a civic context that encourages them to view foundational moral principles from that other's perspective. All of these benefits have been well recognized by educators and educational theorists. Moreover, the "other" in question is not always a representative of a different religious system. Study of the Bible, for example, can generate recognition of an "other within" as well as an "other without," as readers develop recognition of interpretive diversity *within* their own traditions. And, with the recognition of the religious other and of the other within one's own religion, religion courses can contribute to strengthening the bonds of civil society and the enhancement of public life in a liberal society.

However, as we have seen, religion courses are also subject to considerable misuse even by well-intended teachers. Biblical characters and events are treated as if they were confirmed historical accounts, and hence a literal reading of the Bible is promoted, either wittingly or unwittingly. Universal moral lessons are drawn from carefully selected passages of the Bible. Favored interpretations masquerade as the one and only literal truth. The biblical account of ancient Israel is used to promote, as absolute and unquestionable fact, American exceptionalism.

Of course, debates over the purposes and values of courses in religion and

Bible should take place. Yet these debates are often consumed by constitutional issues and especially by the question whether a course is religiously neutral or not. But, we have shown, legal and constitutional questions are not the only ones at stake. Instead of prioritizing "neutrality" as the only principle of educational legitimacy, we believe that a conception of civic "public" should be an important consideration in public-school courses in religion.

Frequently, religion courses respond to the local conditions as educators in a school district perceive them. By local conditions, we mean more than the religious makeup of the community. In our research, teachers usually had an accurate impression of the religious composition of their school community, at least at a given moment in time. Nevertheless, what they discussed with us had to do with the educational and professional aspirations of their students, their social and economic prospects, their central moral challenges, and the degree to which the community values were reflected in the curriculum.

It is necessary for educators to take into account that communities in the United States are not static, but are part of a fluid landscape that is changing in many directions simultaneously. A religion course can help students integrate more fully into their communities, but the course must not explicitly privilege one segment of the community at the expense of others. Moreover, these courses must not just mirror an existing idea of a static community; they must also anticipate the evolution of an emerging public. With this in mind, religion courses, whether in world religions or in Bible, can help students to imagine themselves as members of that public that is coming into existence around them, both in their own schools and in their wider communities. This is best accomplished when courses are taught with student growth foremost in mind.

EDUCATION AS MEDIATION

In a liberal society, the mark of an *educational* exchange should be that the subject matter is purposefully mediated for the sake of growth. For example, the student who intuits the correct answer in math may nonetheless be asked to explain the process by which he or she arrived at it as a way to provide the tools for future, more complex problems. The literature teacher may begin by asking the students whether they enjoyed the poem or story and may even try to find works that he or she knows will have an immediate appeal. Yet the teacher's "why did you like it" follows the student's "I liked it" and initiates a probe intended to en-courage the student to explain his response in light of the text itself. We found that one of the distinguishing features in our different religion courses was the complexity of the mediation, and that this mediation was influenced by the ex-tent to which teachers were self-consciously aware of the influence of their own religious commitments on their teaching. The more self-conscious the teachers, the more likely they were to aid self-awareness in their students. As mediation becomes more complex, the educational potential of a course becomes greater. And as students develop their ability to mediate their own preunderstanding of text and tradition, they can take a larger role in consciously shaping their own development. When this occurs, the aim of the course shifts from simple litera-cy to an important component of a liberal, self-forming, education—autonomy. Here we see the beginning of a liberal education where students become aware of and reflect on the elements of their own formation.

An education for self-reflection is a reasonable horizon for religion courses and certainly could serve to guide more advanced educational effort. Here dis-continuities, as well as continuities, within texts and between traditions become an important background element of the course, shaping the way in which ma-terial is presented to students and providing opportunities for avenues of inqui-ry to emerge. This horizon calls for a level of biblical sophistication that many teachers, and, ironically, often those who are the most biblically literate, lack. Yet we think it provides one of the most promising ways to engage students in an important educational experience and to alert them to the kind of plurality and fluidity that are marks of a modern, global society.

THE TENSION BETWEEN SCHOLARSHIP AND HIGH-SCHOOL TEACHING

Teachers need to be aware that religious texts and traditions contain disrup-tions and discontinuities if they are to avoid misleading students to believe that there is more unity within a religious tradition or a religious text than is actually warranted. Unfortunately, many teachers treat the Bible as a single, undiffer-entiated text—an assumption that is actually reinforced when different stories are either seen as a part of one big story or when each story is investigated as a unitary literary object in its own right, without examining tensions and changes across different parts of the biblical text, and without seeing it as rooted in the temporal concerns of a specific group at a specific time. In each of these cases students are denied the opportunity to see the progressions, as well as the disjunctions, that are actually a part of the Bible.

The same can be said for world-religion courses where each religious tradition is often looked at as a static thing that the subject must come to understand in its oneness. There are some exceptions to this, as for example, when the Sunni and Sufi are distinguished in Islam or Reform and Orthodox Judaism, but the idea that a religious tradition exists as a static object is often the governing metaphor, serving to frame the instruction. This sets up the teaching dynamic. World-religion classes define the object of the course in terms of systems of belief and practice that while varying over time nevertheless embody coherent and distinct views of the world, goals for their practitioners, and corresponding social and ethical obligations. The applicability of the term "religion" can be disputed in some cases (e.g., Confucianism), and many scholars would extend the concept of "religion" to include other communities of practice not typically defined in these terms (e.g., communism, fascism). While allowing for this variance, a stable conception of religion as comprised of identifiable beliefs (expressed either in systematic doctrine or mythological narrative), ritual practices that express and enact these beliefs, and moral codes is shared in world-religion classes. What is lost is the sense of an evolutionary dynamic within religious traditions themselves.[1]

This conception of religion has been strenuously challenged in academic investigations as insufficient to account for numerous types of practice and as already implicitly encoding a Christianized conception of the nature and function of religion. For example, it is unclear whether "belief" necessarily constitutes a dimension of religion, or that religions must promote a goal for individual adherents, or that they must prescribe a moral code. There is, consequently, some disjuncture between contemporary academic discussion on the phenomenon of religion and the presuppositions that are embedded in a typical high-school world-religions class.

Let us not, however, get too carried away with the implications of this analysis for the classroom. It is important to keep in view that an aim of such classes is not primarily to undertake a critical examination of the *concept* of "religion," but rather to help students map out the diversity (including the similarities) of practices that are widespread across numerous cultural/religious systems

throughout the world. As such, one primary aim in many such classes is to promote "understanding," with the presumption that through the process of the
course the student will encounter a way of engaging the world that is radically
"other." Yet this otherness might be unfrozen to some educational advantage by
acknowledging plurality and fluidity within traditions.

In world-religions courses the conception of "understanding" itself is susceptible to two significant differences. The first, and more predominant, way of interpreting "understanding" is as empathy.[2] The basic theory at work is that authentic
knowledge of an unfamiliar object includes at least some degree of identification
with it. Consequently, the ethos in these courses is to bridge apparent differences
by prompting students to identify durable similarities of structure among world
religious traditions, even if those similarities might be masked by more apparent
differences. In this context, empathy functions as both a means to an end (a more
profound assessment of the traditions under study) and also as an end itself (using the religious other to enhance a student's capacity for empathetic identification). Success in the course is to some degree measured by the ability of the
student to identify something of him- or herself in the religious other. This empathetic model turns on understanding as involving a movement of identifying
one's own self with a perceived other. The cost is that most all of the differences
between religions, including important frictions, must be smoothed over. Thus
the picture that the students get emphasizes some ideal of a religion harmonized
with other religions and divorced from conflict and engagement.

In counterpoint to this dynamic of identification, some world-religion
teachers place more emphasis on distancing moves. They prioritize acquisi-
tion of skill in employing critical academic vocabulary—such as "ritual" or
"mythology"—that rhetorically separates the investigator from the object of
investigation. One implicit aim of this approach is to counter the possibility
that empathy will lead to a minimization of difference. From this perspective,
honoring difference is sine qua non for authentic respect and teachers adopting
this stance in the classroom will be less likely to embed perceived differences in a
more embracing structure of similarity. This distancing model of understanding
does not so much contest the goal of empathy as it seeks to regulate it so as not
to overwhelm the real differences across belief systems. Whereas the first model
aims at a dynamics of identification that moderate the distance across religions,
here the aim is to help students distance themselves from their own beliefs only
to the extent required to cultivate what we call a "respectful empathy."

The same polarity between identification and critical distance can operate with respect to Bible classes, but with substantially different implications for the teacher's role, the conception of the object of study in the course, and the moral and cognitive outcomes intended for the student. The Bible has been the subject of over three centuries of critical scholarly investigation. One of the chief results of this cumulative enterprise has been increasing doubt whether the text encodes a single set of beliefs, a set of ritual practices, or a single ethical perspective. Study of the Bible's text has challenged the notion of a biblical "religion," upon which platform Judaism and Christianity subsequently developed. For many biblical scholars, the Bible is not a witness to a single "religion," but is a collection of texts that reflects a diversity of literary and cultural practices undertaken by various communities over a period of a millennium. The religions of Judaism and Christianity, from this perspective, emerge as particular modes of reception rather than as structures erected on the foundation of the text. Moreover, these modes of reception developed in dispute and dialogue with other potential interpretations. As a result, a biblical scholar would not typically see either Christianity or Judaism as an organic extension of a singular biblical worldview, but rather as a negotiation of possible interpretive strategies.

This critical perspective on the Bible has taken centuries to coalesce and does not rest in any one particular methodology. Individual elements of biblical criticism that have been folded into this perspective have been, and will continue to be, contested.[3] Nevertheless, the well-established practices of biblical criticism bear an important implication for our study, which appears precisely at the point of the polarity between identification and distancing. Thus, one task of biblical scholarship is to identify and emphasize *discontinuities* between the present-day reader and the biblical text. Those discontinuities manifest themselves at three separate levels. First, the present structure of individual biblical texts preserves the residues of disputes among various communities for authoritative control over those communities' originating traditions. Second, the inclusion of these individual texts into canonical collections attests to disputes over the appropriate maintenance of a community's legacy.[4] Finally, there is a discontinuity of social and cultural presuppositions between the traditional faith communities that have identified the Bible as their foundational document and the originating conditions in which the biblical texts were produced.[5] The overall effect is that biblical scholarship shapes an arena in which the Bible is distant from the concerns and presuppositions of modern readers. If this result were incorporated directly into a classroom, it might alienate students from their own received faith commitments.

By contrast, an important rationale, sometimes but not always explicit, for initiating Bible classes in high schools turns on a move of identification, one which posits a continuous descent of core values and beliefs from ancient Israel to modern America. This continuity is typically defined either in concrete institutional terms as the Bible as foundational to the American constitution (e.g., the Ten Commandments) or more broadly in terms of the Bible as the source for distinctively Western values (e.g., freedom and dignity of the individual). In either formulation, the argument of advocates for Bible courses is that authentic self-knowledge, both individual and collective, requires a degree of "biblical literacy." Students are then to achieve this knowledge both by an act of cultural retrieval and by means of an empathetic assimilation of their situations to those that appear in biblical narratives. A teacher might, for example, encourage a student to see the wellspring of those elements of the civil rights movement that are most uniformly approved in the United States in Martin Luther King Jr.'s retrieval of the prophetic tradition of Israel. This is achieved by connecting two disparate cultural events into a linear structure by means of a proposition derived from biblical narratives ("the God of Israel supports the liberation of the oppressed"). The second movement of identification, however, is no less significant. In this case, a teacher might encourage a student to identify his or her own situation with a circumstance in biblical narratives (Israel's experience of oppression, David's need of forgiveness). In both cases, as in a world-religion class, the teacher seeks to negotiate the potential otherness of the text by appeal to a direct commonality or by embedding separate events within an explanatory framework that points to similarities. This identity is often defended on the grounds that it can provide students with a spiritual and moral template that will help them become good people and good citizens, but which often reinforce the largely taken for granted moral code of a given Christian community, and its understanding of the correct way to read the Bible. In the early chapters of this book, we explored pedagogical moves that aim to reinforce the claim of seamless continuity between the values of ancient Israel and those of the founders of United States. They do so, however, by concealing the interpretive opportunities Bible presents and the discontinuities between the "destiny" of ancient Israel and the intent of the founders of the American republic.

The study of the Bible as literature can help students to open the interpretive opportunities that Bible History courses often close. Literary study imposes its own critical vocabulary that potentially opens distance between the student and the object of study. To treat the Bible as literature can constrain and regulate an uncritical identification. It becomes also possible for teachers to inculcate a respect for the otherness of the biblical world without collapsing the historical distance of present-day readers from biblical narrative and poetry. If so, it may be the case that both world religion and Bible classes could structure the process of learning by a dynamic of identification and distancing.

It is at this point, however, that the distinctive character of biblical scholarship becomes problematic for the high-school Bible class, and where the tension between the aims of academic understanding and socialization becomes manifest. If, as discussed earlier, the central thrust of biblical scholarship over the centuries has been to undermine either a textual or ideological unity to the Bible, then any move toward identification of the reader with a biblical worldview becomes complicated. This is because from the perspective of biblical scholarship the origins of individual biblical texts and of the biblical canons of individual faith communities are themselves rooted in a process of dispute and contest of authority within and between ancient communities. This makes the act of interpretation, which we described in chapter 6, more complicated and potentially more subversive than it may appear at first. Diversity is not simply an effect caused by competing *appropriations* of the Bible, or even by competing but equally reasonable interpretations of a single and uniform text. Rather, diversity is indeed *generative of* the biblical texts as we possess them.

If a teacher were seriously to engage students with this perspective, the mode of interaction of the reader with the text becomes less one of identification and more one of critical mapping of a terrain marked as much by competition and dispute as much as continuity and uniformity. In part, this is what Mr. Watson was doing when he described to his students some of the factors that went into the construction of the Bible, although he did this largely without exploring points of tension or discontinuity. But this is difficult when students and parents are likely to approach the subject with strong intellectual and emotional residues that support the view that the Bible is a unified and coherent text. Courses that critically map the biblical texts showing discontinuities and disjunctions are fragile and susceptible to highly discomforting breaches of students' preconceptions. Hence the one-to-one correspondence between what scholars know and what teachers can do may be problematic.

As a consequence of the fact that this residue is weaker in the case of world-religion classes, the existing body of scholarship can be accessed with less interference to support a polarity between identification and distancing. For this reason, we believe that politically it may be easier for some teachers to represent plurality and fluidity in world-religion courses than in Bible courses.

All too frequently the divide between high-school teaching and scholarship is wide indeed. For the most, part high-school teachers are not aware of the discontinuities that scholars reveal, and scholars in turn have little patience for the institutional messiness in which high-school teachers operate. Not only is it difficult to introduce courses in Bible or world religion into many schools, it is also all too easy to introduce them in others, but for the wrong reasons. It is also useful to note that this disruption between scholarship and high-school teaching is not confined to religion or Bible courses. Historians have long challenged traditional textbook treatments of American history, which also tend to depict one more or less continuous movement toward freedom and inclusiveness. Much of history is used to promote an uncritical identity with country and patriotism.

Yet, as Aristotle observed when initiating the idea of a public education, a public education has two purposes: to develop civic friendship, or what we might call today social cohesion, and also to develop the virtue of reason, or what we would likely call today critical thinking. The first calls for a kind of patriotism—one in which individuals have an understanding of and commitment to one another and not just to some abstraction called a state. The second calls for a robust, but civil dialogue between these individuals regarding what to count as a common good and the values required to sustain liberal democracies, including the extension of these rights to those who think and believe differently than oneself. Religion and Bible courses can serve to further this dialogue if they are able to communicate the openness and fluidity to phenomena often perceived as fixed and unchanging.

SUGGESTIONS

We are not in any position to recommend whether any given school or district should teach about religion, or if it does, what course or courses it should adopt. Our sample cases, however, allow a few suggestions and some concluding observations. Of the Bible courses we observed, the Bible as Literature is the most academically promising with the least potential for explicit violation of the norms of educational legitimacy. The disciplinary structure of the course enables it to serve the function of interrupting the seamless continuity between classroom and community, particularly by instilling a measure of detachment from the object of study. This process of interruption (by the teacher) and detachment (by the student) is quite useful in cultivating an ability to see an "other" as a legitimate fellow interpreter of the Bible. The Bible as Literature in this way can support recognition of an internal diversity within faith communities or in the use of the Bible outside any faith tradition. Granted, the risk that some students might want to hijack this material for devotional or propaganda purposes is real. In our observation of Ms. Smith's class, however, we noted that discussions frequently moved from literary to theological categories, without any group of students monopolizing the conversation. Students in that class, moreover, articulated appreciation for developing a vocabulary and rules of discourse by which they might undertake these theological tangents with others who might not share their experience or perspective. Moreover, we saw that an experienced teacher like Mr. Bradley was able to use the attempted hijacking to teach important lessons about civil and civic engagement. The chief difficulty is finding ways to educate teachers to be self-conscious about the character of their own religious belief and about how to provide students with an open forum for understanding the literature of the Bible through the disciplinary categories of literary study (genre, character, plot, motif, etc.).

Courses in Bible History are the most problematic type among our samples. The chief difficulty in these courses is the operating presumption that the Bible is a "history textbook" that provides *unmediated* access to the historical events of the nation of Israel and/or the early Christian community. Moreover, these courses are most frequently preferred by communities that wish to reinforce the values of the dominant segments of the community through an affirmation of biblical authority. This operative presumption of unmediated transmission of events is closely connected to the validation desired of biblical, and hence religious communal, authority. The best disciplinary tools to interrupt this uncritical continuity between classroom and community are to be found, as discussed in chapter 5, in the methodology for use of primary sources in the investigation of history. Primary-source investigation is widely undertaken in good high-school history courses, but in our observation and curriculum review there is reluctance to apply this critical approach to the Bible. We would recommend, consequently, that schools that choose this approach to a Bible course either treat the Bible under the canons of primary-source investigation or find another means to open the classroom to diversity within and between faith traditions. One such means to do so might be to include elements of a Bible and Its Influence course alongside the Bible History curriculum.

There is no reason to ignore the influence of the Bible and religion throughout the history of the United States, including the influence of Christianity on some of the Founders. Problems arise when students are told that Christianity was a unique influence, separating it from the general culture of the Enlightenment, and the other streams of intellectual inquiry, such as deism, in which the nation's founders participated. Bible Influence courses are certainly right to emphasize the importance of the Bible as an inspirational text and the role it played in events such as the American Revolution, the abolition movement, the civil rights movement, and other social-justice movements. Yet there are other strands in the Bible as well—other themes that are less in accord with modern norms—which have been used to justify slavery, imperialism, and the subjugation of women. These too should be acknowledged. The tendency to ignore the interpretive tensions in the Bible and to present it as a seamless, consistent web is a misrepresentation. A more accurate alternative would allow students to see how the Bible worked for different readers at different times. This alternative would allow students to gain some perspective on their own times, on their particular traditions, and on contemporary problems and to entertain the idea that the Bible's very openness demands that it cannot be the final arbiter of public policy.

World religion can be of great importance in an ever more globalizing world, where religious differences are part and parcel of both the international and the national discourse. Here we suggest only that teachers should not distort the real differences between religions for the sake of revealing some elusive, harmonious essence. If students are to learn to relate to different standpoints, then they need be able to entertain the possibility that there may well be some differences that are not reducible to an essentially similar set of core values. Certainly, respect is an important consideration in these courses, but ultimately the object of respect is not some abstraction called Islam, Judaism, Buddhism, or any other tradition. It is real people—Muslims, Jews, Christians, or Buddhists, agnostics and atheists who hold to (or do not) certain beliefs, commitments, and practices.[6] To respect these human beings is to honor their right to hold these beliefs, to act on these commitments, and to engage with others in these practices. It is also to honor the rights of others to reject these beliefs, commitments, and practices. Thus, knowledge is an ingredient of respect, but it should not be distorted for the sake of respect. Having said this, world religion can be a very important aspect of establishing a welcoming school climate, and given the increasing diversity of many schools, this suggests that courses in world religion be taught earlier, rather than later, in the curriculum.

CONCLUSION

Religion, as a humanities subject, does not seek obedience, character development, deepening faith, or even religious tolerance. While many of these traits are appropriate outcomes of all education, the humanities require that schools respect and enhance a student's autonomy and judgment, that—while requiring respect for others—it not overly specify what moral behavior or character development might mean, and that it not predefine the outcome ahead of time, independently of an engagement with the student. In church, mosque, temple, or synagogue, at home and in religious gatherings, religion can be taught primarily for both faith goals and for unreflective character goals—but perhaps these are not the best goals to advance the distinctive mission of public schools.

As a humanistic subject, the task of the study or religion is to enhance the student's capacity for understanding, appreciating, and, yes, evaluating religious movements, systems, beliefs, and claims. The faith of the humanities teacher is that students will develop this capacity by acquiring adequate and accurate information, and informed understanding, and then by developing the relevant interpretive, analytic, and critical skills by which to apply this information. The difficulty of doing this is one reason why many schools fear that religion is the third rail of public education and why they avoid the topic, leaving the teaching of religion to the different religious traditions. However, in a multireligious pluralistic democracy, this avoidance may well produce citizens who have very limited and quite distorted understanding of one another, as well as of their own traditions.

There is a great tendency where religion courses are taught to use them for either their perceived moral value as builders of good character or because they satisfy the interests of some segment of the community. We have problems with religion courses that are taught solely for these purposes. This is not just because there may be some legal questions entailed in identifying religion with the moral order, but more importantly because the path to development, both individual and collective, is presented as closed. Rather than students developing their interpretive, analytic, and critical skills for membership in a public that is continually under construction, and whose trajectory remains open to redefinition through critical engagement, they are presented with a completed blueprint that needs only to be followed.

We need to be clear here. Our objection is not to the teaching of character development. Schools do this all the time. And this they must do. When students are taught to take turns, to stand in line, to help others, to clean their desk, to maintain order, to raise their hand for recognition, to play fairly, and honor other students for their performance, effort, or perseverance, they are being taught moral character traits. Religion courses should not be much different in this regard than other courses. Nor are we arguing against the idea that a religion course might well reflect some religious traditions more than others. Indeed, one element of the humanities, as we have shown, is recognition, and in teaching religion it is almost inevitable that some religious traditions will receive more attention than others.[7]

The basic problem is the tendency to place these courses in nonhumanistic frames, where the skills needed to shape an open collective future are blocked and the moral universe is presented as closed. Our vision, and we do realize that it is a vision, is that the civic task of public education is to create a discursive and critical public. While it is certainly a vision, it is not an unrealizable one. As we have shown, elements of this vision are already present in a number of existing religion courses. These elements remain some distance from the complete vision that we believe civic education requires in religiously diverse democracies, but we do believe that they could serve as guides to a civil discussion about the role of public education in advancing public formation across religious differences.

Method and the Schools Included in the Study

Our study is an exercise in applied philosophy of education that employs ethnographic, historical, and biblical scholarship to understand the teaching of courses with religious content in public schools. We aim first to understand what teachers are trying to do and why they are trying to do it. Our goal is, in part, to understand their goals, but this is not our only purpose. This investigation is an exercise in *Vernunft* as much as in *Verstehen*. We seek to understand not only what they are doing, but, more significantly, what they think they ought to be doing—how they believe their professional roles as teachers should be fulfilled—and by means of this deeper understanding to reconstruct the rationale for teaching religion courses in public schools that accords with the idea of education in a religiously pluralistic democratic society, one that goes beyond the vague goal of religious literacy.

As our aim was to engage the participants in an act of rational reconstruction, it was necessary for us to contribute to a setting where they become self-reflective about their teaching in a normative way. Thus, against normal rules of ethnography, we wanted them to see us, at least implicitly, as bearers of pedagogical authority, and there is little doubt that our standing as university professors was on their minds. They were both pleased that we had selected them and they were concerned to communicate to us that they understood the meaning of "good teaching." Their perception of our standing then served as a catalyst to help them reflect on what they are doing and how they might do it differently. Did they change as a result? We suspect that some did, but such was not our point. By projecting what they *believe* we were thinking about their teaching, our presence as pedagogical authorities assisted them in shedding the light of reflection on their own practices, while it helped us articulate a more explicit normative frame. In other words, by becoming their vicarious normative template we become their partner and they ours in the construction of criteria that should govern classroom teaching about religion.

This is similar in one very restricted way to the relationship between the analyst and analysand in the sense that we serve as a template upon which teachers can project their own ideas of good teaching. Even though we take a nonjudgmental stance, teachers project on to us the norms of the educational and scholarly communities and use that projection to refine their own ideas of good teaching. We do not use this approach to trick them. We use it to see just what professional references they implicitly take to be a model of acceptable teaching. Of course, as we use their self-reflection, which is delivered largely as responses to questions like: "Why did you do that?" or "Why did you ask that question?" we add additional refinements of our own.

By serving as a catalyst to promote self-reflection about their own practice, the teachers allow us to see the norms that make up the ideal and internalized contours of the teaching profession. In return, by making these norms conscious and collectively available we hope to strengthen the professional authority of teachers and to enable them to use that authority to better inform the communal authority of school boards and the administrative/legal authority of superintendents. We want to take what is often implicit and unarticulated in the self-understanding of teachers and to help them to articulate it so that it becomes a part of their collective, professional consciousness. Unlike reporters or ethnographers, we want our presence to influence the reporting of our subjects so that they can make visible to us the contours of their professional community. Our job then is to refine this assemblage of off-the-cuff remarks, excuses, apologies, and critical reflections into generalized norms that the profession can refer to in addressing the expectations of the community and the authority of school boards and administrators.

SCHOOLS AND COMMUNITIES INCLUDED IN THE STUDY

Tearville is located in a coastal state in the South, in rural Tapscott County, which has a population of approximately 150,000 and median household income slightly more than $50,000.[1] Surveys by the Association of Religion Data Archives (ARDA) identify more than 100 evangelical Protestant congregations and over 80 more mainline Protestant congregations. The county is also home to two Catholic churches, but the estimated populations of Jews, Muslims, Mormons, and Baha'i are minuscule.[2] Even though only 50 percent of the county's residents are identified as adherents to any religious community, Baptists and Methodists represent the dominant religious culture—accounting for almost half of the number of congregations, and more than half of the total adherents in the county.

Ridge County, which is located in a rural county in a South Central state, presents a social/economic and cultural/religious landscape similar to Tapscott County. The county's population is somewhat more than 20,000, with a median household income close to $30,000. The dominant religious culture in Ridge County is even more strongly evangelical than that of Tapscott: ARDA identifies more than sixty evangelical congregations, and only one small Catholic church in the county. The most prominent denomination in Ridge County is the Church of Christ, which is noted for a strong tradition of biblical literalism.

The third school participating in this study, Jordan County, is a rural county in a mid-Atlantic state with a population around 120,000 and a median household income about $50,000. ARDA identifies more "mainline" Protestant congregations in Jordan than evangelical denominations, but our survey of the literature of these mainline churches suggests that they stand toward the conservative end of their denominations. In recent years, the county has begun to experience widening religious diversity, perhaps related to the county's relative proximity to the state's capital city (about an hour's drive) and also the presence of a small liberal arts college within the county. The college, although historically affiliated with a Christian church, supports both a Hillel foundation and a Buddhist meditation group. More broadly, the county is home to a number of Catholic churches, a Coptic Orthodox congregation that occupies the property of a previous "mainline" church, a long-standing Jewish community, and a burgeoning presence of New Age groups. ARDA data suggest that religious identity in Jordan County might be somewhat diminishing. From 1980 to 2000, the county has experienced a 6 percent decrease in adherents to religious congregations despite an increase in its total population of more than 10 percent.

The other three schools are located in communities with much diminished evangelical Protestant cultural authority. The first school, Lakeside High, is located in a small city in the Midwest, slightly beyond comfortable commuting distance from a major urban center. The county boasts a population of more than 500,000, with a median household income above $65,000. In contrast to the previous counties discussed, Lakeside's district is majority Catholic. The county, nevertheless, is religiously diverse: a wide range of Protestant churches—Pentecostal, liberal, and evangelical—are well represented, and these congregations share the county with a vigorous Greek Orthodox community, two synagogues, several mosques and Islamic centers, and a few small Baha'i household congregations.

The final two schools in the study both offer world-religion courses. Neither school offers Bible courses, and both of them present world religions as a preferable alternative in their communities. The first, Johnson High School, teaches a one-semester class in world religion, and includes nonliterary and small-scale religions, as well as the more well-known world traditions with their literary canons. The school is located in a religiously and ethnically diverse professional suburb of a large Midwest urban center. The county has a population of almost 750,000, with a median household income of almost $80,000. The county's religious landscape is notable for a high density of synagogues, mosques, and Islamic centers, along with the broad spectrum of Christian communities. The high school has been designated as a model of excellence; it is often visited by educators from other communities around the country, and Johnson High has developed a regular program for these visitors. This school is also unique among our participating sites in that its world-religions course was initiated a few years ago in response to students who in a questionnaire suggested this addition to the curriculum.

The final school in the study, Eastland High, is also located in a wealthy suburban township adjacent to a major urban center in the Midwest. The township has a population of approximately 45,000, with a median household income over $100,000. Data on the religious communities in the township could not be isolated from ARDA's county aggregation, but religious diversity was manifest during our visits. The school is in close enough proximity to a Hindu temple to enable an easy class field trip, and representatives from Muslim communities were available for visits to the class. The school offers a number of sections of two elective courses—one course in Western religions, the other in Eastern traditions. The courses were initiated over twenty-five years ago by the current head of the social studies department and are now taught by a team of three teachers, all veterans. This school's social studies program was unique among participating schools in that the department chooses to meet most of its state-mandated requirements *through* electives proposed and developed by their teachers. Eastland, in this way, diminishes the distinction between "elective" and "core" courses.

NOTES

Chapter 1

1. For a superb account of the process of establishing a Bible elective in Odessa, see Chancey, "The Bible, the First Amendment, and the Public Schools in Odessa, Texas," esp. 174–79.

2. Sullivan, "When Would Jesus Bolt: Meet Randy Brinson, the Advanced Guard of the Evangelicals Leaving the GOP"; see also the discussion of Chancey, "Bible Bills, Bible Curricula, and Controversies of Biblical Proportions."

3. Brighouse, *School Choice and Social Justice.*

4. Wexler, "Preparing for the Clothed Public Square: Teaching about Religion, Civic Education and the Constitution."

5. For an extended discussion of autonomy, see Hurka, "Why Value Autonomy?"

6. Noddings, *Educating for Intelligent Belief or Unbelief.*

7. Nord and Haynes, *Taking Religion Seriously Across the Curriculum.*

8. Nash and Bishop, *Teaching Adolescents Religious Literacy in a Post-9/11 World.* True, there could be more in the way of curricular material, but the Pluralism Project at Harvard has been working to correct this deficit and its web page could be of great help to interested teachers: The Pluralism Project: http://pluralism.org/resources/tradition/index. php?trad=3

9. *Abington Township v. Schempp,* 374 U.S. 203 at 225 (1963).

10. Ibid.

11. *Lemon v. Kurtzman,* 403 U.S. 602 (1971) at 612–61: (1) the action must have a "secular purpose;" (2) its principal or primary effect "must be one that neither advances nor inhibits religion;" and finally, (3) it must not foster "excessive government entanglement with religion." The basic principle was enunciated already by Justice Clark in *Abington:* "The test may be stated as follows: what are the purpose and primary effect of the enactment? If either is the advancement or inhibition of religion, the enactment exceeds the scope of legislative power as circumscribed by the Constitution. That is to say that, to withstand

the strictures of the Establishment Clause, there must be a secular legislative purpose and a primary effect that neither advances nor inhibits religion" (374 U.S. 203, 222).

12. For uses of the Lemon test see, for example, *Wiley v. Franklin*, 474 F. Supp. 525 at 531 (E.D. Tenn. 1979), *Herdahl v. Pontotoc County*, 933 F. Supp. 582 at 595 (N.D. Miss. 1996), *Gibson v. Lee County School Board*, 1 F. Supp. 2d 1426 (M.D. Fla. 1998), *Doe v. Human*, 725 F. Supp. 1499 (W.D. Ark 1989) at 1501, *Crockett v. Sorenson*, 568 F. Supp. 1422 (W.D. Va. 1983) at 1429, *Kitzmiller v. Dover Area School District*, 400 F. Supp. 2d 707 at 712 (M.D. Pa. 2005), 9. (For reservations and dissatisfaction with the Lemon test see, for example, *County of Allegheny v. American Civil Liberties Union*, 492 U.S. 573 (1989), suggesting an "endorsement" test instead. The two tests, however, are not exclusive, and both involve examination of the purpose and effect of a particular practice; see, for example, *Doe v. Porter*, Memorandum at 9. For trenchant critique of the Lemon test, see Michael McConnell "Religious Freedom at a Crossroads," esp. 118–20, 128–31, who nevertheless also rejects the "Endorsement test" as a substitute for Lemon.

13. Justice Brennan wrote in his concurrence: "The holding of the Court today plainly does not foreclose teaching *about* the Holy Scriptures or about the differences between religious sects in classes in literature or history" (*Abington v. Schempp*, 374 U.S. at 300 [Brennan, concurring]). Justice Goldberg was even more explicit in his concurrence: "It seems clear to me . . . that the Court would recognize the propriety of . . . teaching *about* religion, as distinguished from the teaching *of* religion in the public schools" (ibid. at 306 [Goldberg, concurring]). For an excellent review of the legal history of the terminology of teaching "about" religion see Wexler, "Preparing for the Clothed Public Square," 1172–90.

14. Vickery and Cole, *Intercultural Education in American Schools*, 158–62.

15. See, for example, Weigle, "Public Education and Religion." For a critique of this turn in religious instruction, see Prothero, *Religious Literacy*, 111–14.

16. Vickery and Cole, *Intercultural Education*, xv.

17. Among the several commissions appointed and reports compiled, we have particularly used: American Council on Education, *The Relation of Religion to Public Education* (cited here to *Religious Education* 42 [1947]:129–65); idem, *The Function of the Public Schools in Dealing with Religion*; National Education Association, *Moral and Spiritual Values in the Public Schools*; and American Association of School Administrators, *Religion in the Public Schools*.

18. American Council on Education, *Relation of Religion to Public Education*, 138–39.

19. Ibid., p. 139.

20. Ibid., 150.

21. Ibid., 147.

22. Education Policies Commission, *Moral and Spiritual Values*, 77 (emphasis in original).

23. Ibid., 78–79.

24. Ibid., 80.

25. More recent declarations reiterate some of these themes. See, for example, National Council for the Social Studies, "Study about Religions in the Social Studies Curriculum": "Knowledge about religions is not only a characteristic of an educated person, but it is also absolutely necessary for understanding and living in a world of diversity." Knowledge, the council holds, of "religious differences and the role of religion in the contemporary world" can "promote understanding and alleviate prejudice," while, "omitting study about religions gives students the impression that religions have not been and are not now part of the human experience." Nord, *Religion and American Education*, and "Religion, Pluralism, and Public Education in America," echoes some of these themes.

26. Cady, "Territorial Disputes: Religious Studies and Theology in Transition," 111. Cady actually disapproves of what he views as support for hegemonic teaching.

27. See, for example, the concise statement of Haynes and Thomas, *Finding Common Ground*, 97–98. These same guidelines are endorsed by the California History–Social Science Curriculum Framework and Criteria Committee, History–Social Science Framework for California Public Schools, 210.

Chapter 2

1. The NCBCPS markets its curriculum, *The Bible in History and Literature*, as suitable for either Bible History or Bible as Literature courses. As discussed in chapter 5 (see the section "*The Bible in History and Literature* as a Curriculum"), however, only one unit of the *BHL* focuses on literary issues and most of the courses that use the curriculum are Bible History.

2. It is part of the "partnership" between the school system and the TBA that the association helps with the interviewing of prospective teachers. David White, one of the teachers hired through this process, identifies one function of the TBA as to "oversee who's hired and who's not."

3. The formation of religious associations to initiate and support Bible or religion classes in public schools is somewhat unusual but it is not unique, nor is it a new phenomenon. The arrangement in Tearville-Tapscott adapts a strategy of support that developed in the 1920s as a means to offer explicitly religious education. In the aftermath of *Abington*, districts relying on Bible associations found themselves under increased scrutiny from nonparticipating religious groups and from civil-rights organizations, such as the American Civil Liberties Union (founded 1917) and later People for the American Way (founded 1981). As a result of this pressure, in the 1970s and 1980s school districts began to absorb many of the components of the Bible association, such as teacher hiring and curriculum development, back into their own systems. Nevertheless, Bible associations do continue to play a significant role in a number of communities, as funding mechanisms but also more broadly as auxiliaries of general community support.

4. *Vaughn v. Reed*, 313 F. Supp. 431 (W. D. Va., 1970), *Wiley v. Franklin*, 468 F. Supp.

133 (E. D. Tenn., 1979), at 136f, *Crockett v. Sorenson*, 568 F. Supp. 1422 (W. D. Va., 1983), at 1431. People for the American Way, *Religion in the North Carolina's Schools*, 6–7, in 1983 raised the financial connection between religious groups and the school district as a point of legal vulnerability.

5. The national survey performed by the National Center for Education Statistics in 2007, which is the most recent year for which the Department of Education compiled this data, estimates that the homeschooling population in the United States numbered about 1.5 million, or 2.9 percent of the total school-age population. *Issue Brief* NCES 2009–30. The statistical data does not distinguish between religious and nonreligious private schools in the community. Our own survey of the local directory of private schools, however, indicated that eight of the nine listed private academies in the district had a Christian orientation. Benjamin Jenkins estimated that private religious academies and homeschooling accounted for 10 percent or more of the total enrollment of school-aged children in the county, indicating that Mr. Jenkins is well-informed of the county's educational demographics. More recent data on homeschool enrollment shows that this number has continued to increase substantially in the years since our visit to the school district.

6. The development of parallel systems among homeschooling families is a widespread tendency: see Hill, "Home Schooling and the Future of Public Education."

7. In the 2007 survey by the National Center for Educational Statistics, the primary reasons parents gave for homeschooling children were "concern about the school environment, to provide religious or moral instruction, and dissatisfaction with the academic instruction available at other schools." Of these three reasons, a plurality of parents (36 percent) identified "to provide religious or moral instruction" as the *most important* reason. See *Issue Brief* NCES 2009–30, 2–3.

8. The "documentary hypothesis" holds that the present form of the Pentateuch results from the editing, or "redaction," of previous narrative strands, or "sources"—identified in scholarship by the sigla J, E, D, and P—each of which are held to reflect the different political and social conditions under which the Pentateuch developed. The roots of this hypothesis can be traced to the eighteenth century, but the theory was given its most enduring presentation and synthesis by Julius Wellhausen in 1878. In the century following Wellhausen, although the documentary hypothesis was critiqued and refined, it remained the foundation for Pentateuchal research. Since the late 1970s, scholars have persistently questioned some of the assumptions underlying the documentary hypothesis, most particularly the identification of independent, continuous narrative strands underlying the Pentateuch, the production of those narratives by a single authorial agency, whether an individual or a "school," and the evolutionary framework presumed by Wellhausen. Nonetheless, no consensus model of Pentateuchal composition has developed as an alternative to the Wellhausen four-source model, and the documentary hypothesis remains as a staple of introductory classes on Hebrew Bible at the college level. For a comprehensive survey of the use and critique of the documentary hypothesis in biblical scholarship, as well as an

assessment of its continued utility, see Nicholson, *The Pentateuch in the Twentieth Century*. Kawashima, "Sources and Redaction," provides a spirited defense of source and redaction theories, as well as a compelling application of this method to the opening chapters of Genesis. In college instruction, the double creation stories of Genesis 1 and 2 often provide a preferred entry into an examination of the documentary hypothesis; see Roncace and Gray, *Teaching the Bible*, esp. 69–73, 77–78, 133–36.

Chapter 3

1. According to the data compiled by the Association of Religion Data Archives (ARDA), only slightly more than 50 percent of the residents of Tapscott County, which administrators identify as part of the Bible Belt, identify themselves as adherents of any religious congregation. School administrators nevertheless perceive a cultural affinity for Christianity in the locality that extends more broadly than simple congregational membership.

2. Noddings, *Educating for Intelligent Belief of Unbelief*.

3. For a brief description and critique of this conception of "historical criticism" and the tools used to achieve this aim see Barton, *The Nature of Biblical Criticism*, 31–68.

4. *Gibson v. Lee County School Board*, 1 F. Supp. 2d 1426 (M. D. Fla., 1998) at 1434: "This Court too finds it difficult to conceive how the account of the resurrection or of miracles could be taught as secular history" (citing *Wiley v. Franklin*, 474 F. Supp. 525).

5. *Herdahl v. Pontotoc County School Dist.*, 933 F. Supp. 582 (N. D. Miss., 1996) at 594.

6. Teaching Genesis as "actual literal history" was one of the points identified by Judge Biggers in his opinion enjoining the Pontotoc County School District from continuing its "Biblical History of the Middle East" course, *Herdahl v. Pontotoc County School Dist.*, 933 F. Supp. 582 (N. D. Miss., 1996) at 594, 596. See also *Doe v. Human*, 725 F. Supp. 1499 (W. D. Ark., 1989) at 1501: "She also taught the children that the Bible is the word of God, and that the creation story in Genesis, indeed the whole Bible, was literally true."

7. *The One Year Chronological Bible. The Entire New International Version in 365 Daily Readings*.

8. We use quotation marks here to signal that the Bible does not label the stories as miracles.

9. The emphasis was in the original.

10. Biblical scholars might detect a certain ambiguity in Black's reference to a single "biblical version" of the parting of the sea. Most commentators have judged that the account of Israel's deliverance at the sea is composed from multiple sources, which the present state of the text preserves in a manner that does not completely eliminate the tensions between them. For one discussion of the issues presented by the account see Childs, *The Book of Exodus*, 215–30. For an example of how a teacher might develop these tensions to perform pedagogical work, see Roncace and Gray, *Teaching the Bible*, 115–17.

11. In an interview with Mr. Black, we raised this distinction, and he allowed that the miracle disclaimer "generally" referred to the explanation of the event and not to its occurrence.

Chapter 4

1. Taylor, *Multiculturalism and the Politics of Recognition*, 36.

2. See, for example, *Doe v. Human*, 725 F. Supp. 1503 (W. D. Ark, 1989), in which the judge, employing the Lemon test, rejected the defense made by the Gravette, Arkansas public schools for its Bible program as aimed to "building character, forming moral values, and developing a truly educated person" on the grounds that the *principal effect* of the courses was to advance religion through its moral instruction. See also *Herdahl v. Pontotoc County School District*, 933 F. Supp. 482 (N. D. Miss. 1996) 582 at 595, ruling that the school district's Bible class did not possess primarily a secular purpose (as required in the Lemon test), but rather sought "to inculcate students at North Pontotoc into the beliefs *and moral code* of fundamentalist Christianity" (emphasis added). The same judge (596) singled out the usage of materials that proclaimed to teach children the "truths of God's Word" and how to relate it to "everyday experiences" as indicia of the primary effect of the course as the inculcation of religious belief.

3. Milsap reported to us that the girl's tumor was successfully removed by surgery and diagnosed as benign upon biopsy.

4. For an overview of the composition, date, and structure of the Deuteronomistic History see McKenzie, "Deuteronomistic History." As McKenzie, 161, observes, "to the extent that any position in biblical studies can be regarded as the consensus viewpoint, the existence of DH has achieved almost canonical status."

5. See, for example, the study of Peckham, *The Composition of the Deuteronomistic History*.

6. Most scholars also detect a note of optimism in the DH, which does not find expression in Black's and Milsap's recitation of the moral "lesson" for their students.

7. See, for example, Ackroyd, *Exile and Restoration*.

8. See especially von Rad, "The Deuteronomic Theology of History," and *Old Testament Theology*, vol. 1, 334–47; Frank Moore Cross, *Canaanite Myth and Hebrew Epic*, 274–90.

Chapter 5

1. The superintendent reports that 63 percent of the 2007 class at Jordan continued to either a two-year or four-year undergraduate institution. Previous to his arrival in the county, the school averaged 59 percent of its graduates continuing education in the year after graduation.

2. National Council on Bible Curriculum in Public Schools, http://www.bibleinschools.net/Where-This-Has-Been-Implemented.

3. See Chancey, "Textbook Example," 555. An independent survey conducted in 2005 by the Texas Freedom Network identified only eleven schools following the NCBCPS curriculum altogether or in part. See Chancey, *Reading, Writing, & Religion*, 20.

4. On the involvement of Christian reconstructionism and other fundamentalist movements with educational issues see Lugg, "Reading, Writing, and Reconstructionism: The Christian Right and the Politics of Public Education"; and Sara Diamond, *Roads to Dominion.*

5. For a list of the council's directors and members of its advisory board see http://www.bibleinschools.net/About-Us/Board-of-Directors-and-Advisors.

6. The WallBuilders' view of their purpose can be seen at their website: http://www.wallbuilders.com/ABTOverview.asp. BHL, 4, promotes WallBuilders resources for use in the classroom. BHL, 11 recommends teachers to show the WallBuilders' video "Foundations of American Government" to introduce the course.

7. See "National Council on Bible Curriculum," Coral Ridge Ministries Video, August 1, 2004, http://www.coralridge.org/medialibrary/default.aspx?mediaID=1375.

8. BHL, v: "No public school teacher or official should ever endorse, favor, promote, or disfavor, or show hostility to, any particular religion or nonreligious faith. Nothing in this curriculum is intended to violate any provision of the United States Constitution or federal law, any state constitution or state law." BHL, 1 identifies as one of the course objectives: "To inform the student of the importance of religion in world and national history without imposing the doctrine of any particular religious sect." BHL, 124 includes a caution to the teacher in planning a lesson on the Psalms: "(*Note: The instructor must point out that these selections are being reviewed only for their influential literary and poetic qualities, and that the review must not be regarded or treated as a 'devotional' exercise—inappropriate for a classroom setting.)*" (emphasis in original)

9. *Gibson v. Lee County School Board*, 1 F. Supp 2d 1426 (M. D. Fla, 1998). See also the discussion of Chancey, "Textbook Case," 560, with further bibliography. As Chancey notes, the NCBCPS maintains that the *Gibson* decision was not directed at their curriculum, even though the judge's decision is quite clear that it was the refusal of the Bible Curriculum Committee and the school board to accept recommended modifications to the NCBCPS curriculum that precipitated the legal action.

10. See, for example, Banerjee, "District to Settle Bible Suit," *New York Times*, March 6, 2008; the ACLU issued its own press release: http://www.aclu.org/religion-belief/texas-school-board-agrees-stop-teaching-unconstitutional-bible-class-public-schools.

11. See, for example, Wind, "Waterloo Will Not Consider High School Bible Class," October 2008, (Waterloo, Iowa); Elizabeth W. Caroon, "School Board Adopts Bible Class Text," February 2011, (Chesterfield County, Virginia). ACLU attorneys had previously sent the Chesterfield school board a letter alleging that the National Council curriculum

could be subject to legal challenge: Lizama, "ACLU Criticizes Bible Textbook."

12. Schippe and Stetson, eds., *The Bible and Its Influence* (hereafter cited as *BI*); Haney Schafer, *The Bible and Its Influence* (teacher's edition) (hereafter cited as *BI-TE*).

13. The Memphis pilot project was reported in a series of articles by Katherine Cromer in the Memphis *Commercial Appeal:* "Pilot Bible Course to be Offered in All County High Schools," March 23, 2002; "Bible Course Teachers Eager to Do it Right," August 13, 2002; "Prophets Foretold Multitudes in Bible Class, But they Didn't Come," August 20, 2002. See also Haynes, "The Bible in Memphis."

14. Haynes, "From Battleground to Common Ground: Religion in the Public Square of 21st Century America," esp. 97, 100–103.

15. Lowry, "Know Thy Bible."

16. Letter of John C. Hagee to Representative Scott Beason and the Members of the Alabama Legislature, March 12, 2006. Quotes from 2. A PDF file of the letter is posted on the National Council's website.

17. Siegel, "Bible Guide for Public Schools Gets Jewish Okay."

18. The placement of literary study to the periphery of interests for the BHL is further indicated by the prefatory letter of Tracey Kiesling to instructors, who advises that the core of the curriculum is set by "the Pentateuch, the Exodus, Psalms and Proverbs, the Gospels and Acts" (BHL, 9).

19. Letter of Cynthia Dunbar, Terri Leo, Gail Lowe, Barbara C. Cargill to administrators and school-board members, September 15, 2008. The letter, printed on State Board of Education letterhead, is reproduced on the National Council Website: http://www.bibleinschools.net/images/texasletter/.

20. *History-Social Science Framework for California Public Schools*, 218–20.

21. See, for example, 61, assigning the students the task to "diagram the Genesis account of the seven days of creation," harmonizing the variant progression of elements in Genesis 1 and 2. See also, 124, restricting classroom discussion of Job to chapters 38–41, which bypasses the problematic suffering of the protagonist in favor of the majestic theophany.

22. *BI-TE*, 18.

23. *BI-TE*, 20.

24. The textbook discusses Martin Buber's interpretation of the sacrifice of Isaac, which it refers to by the traditional Jewish title, *akedah* ("binding") (61); includes Jewish imagery (e.g., frontispiece of a contemporary American Haggadah [70]); and includes a feature that relates the Israelite exile to contemporary Middle Eastern political disputes (108–9).

25. For examples of recognition of African-American interpretive traditions and reception of the Bible see BI, 10 (Martin Luther King Jr.), 67 (spirituals as interpretations of the Exodus), and an extensive feature on African-American traditions of liberation (88–89).

26. This point is raised by Steven McKenzie in his review of the *Bible and its Influence* , *SBL Forum*, http://www.sbl-site.org/publications/article.aspx?articleId=465.

27. Norris, "Don't Mess with Texas . . . Textbooks!" WND commentary, March 15, 2010, http://www.wnd.com/2010/03/127935/.

Chapter 6

1. We put quotation marks here to indicate that while this understanding of reading is strongly associated with the Protestant legacy, not all Protestant denominations completely accept this understanding.

2. Hirsch Jr., *Cultural Literacy: What Every American Needs to Know.*

3. For an example of a "recall" exercise for the entire span of the Abraham cycle (Genesis 12–25) see BHL, 67–69.

4. Holzer, "Allowing the Text to do its Pedagogical Work."

5. Bekoff and Pierce, *Wild Justice,* 132.

6. Noddings, *Educating for Intelligent Belief and Unbelief.*

Chapter 7

1. Moore, *Overcoming Religious Illiteracy,* 27.

2. Brackets added for clarity

3. Our appreciation to Mr. Miller for providing us with samples of anonymous student papers.

Chapter 8

1. Moore, *Overcoming Religious Illiteracy* (37, 39), rightly emphasizes that courses about religion should account for diversity within religious traditions and avoid presenting them as "timeless, uniform, and unchanging systems of belief."

2. Nord, *Religion and American Education* (213–22), makes a sustained case for the necessity of this empathic form of understanding to the study of religion. See also Nord's more recent *Does God Make a Difference* (196) for a restatement of this position.

3. Most visibly, the "documentary hypothesis" for the formation of the Pentateuch and the two- or four-source theory for the Synoptic Gospels.

4. A strongly contested example of this form would be the interpretation of the "Pastoral" epistles, widely understood to be later additions to the Pauline corpus as a means to control legitimate access to the authority of Paul. The creation, however, of the four-gospel canon in Christianity can also be understood as a means to both legitimize and regulate a certain variance in interpretation.

5. This discontinuity is expressed most significantly in the separate interpretive communities of the synagogue and the church, but it is also visible in the bitter disputes that characterize subsequent arguments within Christian communities.

6. Brague, *The Legend of the Middle Ages,* 20.

7. We would differentiate, however, the amount of attention given to a religion from the significance attributed in the course to individual traditions. Nord, *Does God Make a Difference* (115–16), argues that it is justifiable to prioritize traditions according to their

cultural influence and proximity. Prothero, *Religious Literacy* (12–13), appeals to the pervasiveness of Christian rhetoric in American culture and politics as justification for foregrounding Christian literacy in courses on religion. In our view, both of these arguments fail to do justice to the task to make the "strange familiar."

Appendix

1. Population totals, and social and economic data are taken from the 2000 Census, available at the "American Fact Finder" tool of the U.S. Census Bureau: http://factfinder. census.gov/home/saff/main.html?_lang=en. At the time of this writing, community data for the 2010 Census was not yet available.

2. Data for religious demographics are taken from the Association of Religion Data Archives (ARDA): http://www.thearda.com. ARDA divides Protestant congregations into "evangelical" and "mainline" on the basis of the denominational affiliation rather than an analysis of an individual congregation's own views. Thus, ARDA classifies all Presbyterians (USA) and United Methodists as "mainline," although many individual congregations within these denominations reflect strongly evangelical positions, especially on cultural issues. Consequently, ARDA data might overstate the diversity of religious identity in communities. ARDA's reservation, posted on its county demographic tables, concerning the ability to obtain consistent data concerning historically African-American congregations also should be taken into consideration. For these reasons, we use this information only to gain a rough profile of the role of religion in these communities rather than to provide the basis for a detailed ethnographic study.

BIBLIOGRAPHY

Ackroyd, Peter R. *Exile and Restoration: A Study of Hebrew Thought of the Sixth Century B.C.* Philadelphia, PA: Westminster Press, 1968.

American Association of School Administrators, Commission on Religion in the Public Schools, *Religion in the Public Schools*. Washington, D.C.: American Association of School Administrators, 1964.

American Council on Education, Committee on Religion and Education, *The Relation of Religion to Public Education: The Basic Principles*. Washington, D.C.: American Council on Education, 1947. Reprinted in *Religious Education* 42 (1947): 129–65.

American Council on Education. *The Function of the Public Schools in Dealing with Religion: A Report of the Exploratory Study Made by the Committee on Religion and Education*. Washington, D.C.: American Council of Education, 1953.

Bannerjee, Neela. "District to Settle Bible Suit." *New York Times*, March 6, 2008. http://www.nytimes.com/2008/03/06/us/06bible.html?_r=3&oref=slogin&oref=slogin/.

Barton, John. *The Nature of Biblical Criticism*. Louisville, KY: Westminster John Knox Press, 2007.

Bekoff, Marc, and Jessica Pierce. *Wild Justice: The Moral Life of Animals*. Chicago: University of Chicago Press, 2009.

Brague, Remi. *The Legend of the Middle Ages: Philosophical Evaluations of Medieval Christianity, Judaism, and Islam*. Chicago: University of Chicago Press, 2009.

Brighouse, Harry. *School Choice and Social Justice*. Oxford: Oxford University Press, 2000.

Cady, Linell E. "Territorial Disputes: Religious Studies and Theology in Transition." In *Religious Studies, Theology, and the University: Conflicting Maps, Changing Terrain*, edited by Linell E. Cady and Delwin Brown. Albany: State University of New York Press, 2002), 110–25.

Carper, James C. "Pluralism to Establishment to Dissent: The Religious and Educational Context of Home Schooling." *Peabody Journal of Education* 75 (2000): 8–19.

Caroon, Elizabeth W. "School Board Adopts Bible Class Text." *Village News: Chesterfield County*, February 16, 2011. http://www.villagenewsonline.com/node/4098.

Chancey, Mark A. *Reading, Writing & Religion: Teaching the Bible in Texas Public Schools.* Texas Freedom Network, 2006.

Chancey, Mark A. "A Textbook Example of the Christian Right: The National Council on Bible Curriculum in Public Schools." *Journal of the American Academy of Religion* 75 (2007): 554–81.

Chancey, Mark A. "Bible Bills, Bible Curricula, and Controversies of Biblical Proportions: Legislative Efforts to Promote Bible Courses in Public Schools." *Religion & Education* 34 (2007): 28–47.

Chancey, Mark A. "The Bible, the First Amendment, and the Public Schools in Odessa, Texas." *Religion and American Culture* 19 (2009): 169–205.

Childs, Brevard S. *The Book of Exodus: A Critical, Theological Commentary.* Old Testament Library. Philadelphia: Westminster Press, 1974.

Cromer, Katherine. "Pilot Bible Course to Be Offered in All County High Schools." *Commercial Appeal,* March 23, 2002.

Cromer, Katherine. "Bible Course Teachers Eager to 'Do It Right.'" *Commercial Appeal,* August 13, 2002.

Cromer, Katherine. "Prophets Foretold Multitudes in Bible Class, But They Didn't Come." *Commercial Appeal,* August 20, 2002.

Cross, Frank Moore. *Canaanite Myth and Hebrew Epic: Essays in the History of the Religion of Israel.* Cambridge, MA: Harvard University Press, 1973.

Detwiler, Fritz. *Standing on the Premises of God: The Christian Right's Fight to Redefine America's Public Schools.* New York: New York University Press, 1999.

Dewey, John. "Religion and Our Schools." *Hibbert Journal* 6 (July 1908): 796–809.

Diamond, Sara. *Roads to Dominion: Right-wing Movements and Political Power in the United States.* New York: Guilford Press, 1995.

Eck, Diana. *A New Religious America: How a "Christian Country" Has Become the World's Most Religiously Diverse Nation.* New York: HarperCollins, 2002.

Greenawalt, Kent. *Does God Belong in Public Schools.* Princeton, NJ: Princeton University Press, 2005.

Haynes, Charles C., and Oliver Thomas. *Finding Common Ground: A Guide to Religious Liberty in Public Schools.* Nashville: First Amendment Center, 2001.

Haynes, Charles. "From Battleground to Common Ground: Religion in the Public Square of 21st Century America." In *Religion in American Public Life: Living with Our Deepest Differences,* edited by Azizah Y. al-Hibri, Jean Bethke Elshtain, and Charles C. Haynes, 96–136. New York: W. W. Norton, 2001.

Haynes, Charles. "Will New Textbook Bring Peace in School Bible Wars?" October 2, 2005. First Amendment Center. http://www.fac.org/commentary.aspx?id=15859.

Haynes, Stephen R. "The Bible in Memphis." *Religion in the News* 6 (2003). http://www.trincoll.edu/depts/csrpl/rinvol6no1/Bible%20in%20Memphis.htm.

Hill, Paul T. "Home Schooling and the Future of Public Education." *Peabody Journal of Education* 75 (2000): 20–31.

Hirsch, E. D., Jr. *Cultural Literacy: What Every American Needs to Know*. Boston: Houghton Mifflin, 1987. See Hirsch, Core Knowledge Foundation. http://www.coreknowledge.org.

Hirsch, E. D., Jr. *The Knowledge Deficit: Closing the Shocking Gap for American Children*. Boston: Houghton Mifflin, 2006.

History-Social Science Curriculum Framework and Criteria Committee. *History-Social Science Framework for California Public Schools Kindergarten through Grade Twelve*. 2005 Edition with New Criteria for Instructional Materials. Sacramento: California Department of Education, 2005.

Holzer, Elie. "Allowing the Text to Do Its Pedagogical Work: Connecting Moral Education and Interpretive Activity." *Journal of Moral Education* 36 (2007): 497–514.

Hurka, Thomas. "Why Value Autonomy?" *Social Theory and Practice* 13 (1987): 361–82.

Johnson, Luke Timothy. "Textbook Case." *Christian Century*, February 21, 2006, 34–37.

Kaplan, Fred. "Capitalist Casts Bread on Waters; Fund Manager Pays to Promote Study of Bible." *Boston Globe*, November 23, 1998.

Kawashima, Robert S. "Sources and Redaction." In *Reading Genesis: Ten Methods*, edited by Ronald Hendel, 47–70. Cambridge: Cambridge University Press, 2010.

Lester, Emile, and Patrick S. Roberts. *Learning about World Religions in Public Schools: The Impact on Student Attitudes and Community Acceptance in Modesto, Calif*. Nashville: First Amendment Center, 2006.

Levenson, David. "University Religion Departments and Teaching about the Bible in Public Schools: A Report from Florida." *Religious Studies News: AAR Edition*, March 2002, 3, 7, 10. http://www.aarweb.org/teaching/ris/publications.asp. See also the SBL Forum Archive. http://sbl-site.org/publications/article.aspx?articleId=198.

Lizama, Juan Antonio. "ACLU Criticizes Bible Textbook Considered for Class." Newsadvance.com, April 23, 2010). http://www2.newsadvance.com/lifestyles/2010/apr/23/aclu_criticizes_bible_textbook_considered_for_clas-ar-184216/.

Lowry, Rich. "Know Thy Bible." *National Review Online*, October 14, 2005, http://www.nationalreview.com/lowry/lowry200510140801.asp.

Lugg, Catherine A. "Reading, Writing, and Reconstructionism: The Christian Right and the Politics of Public Education." *Educational Policy* 14 (2000): 622–37.

Lugg, Catherine A. "The Christian Right: A Cultivated Collection of Interest Groups." *Educational Policy* 15 (2001): 41–57.

Marsden, George M. *Fundamentalism and American Culture: The Shaping of Twentieth-Century Evangelicalism, 1870–1925*. Oxford: Oxford University Press, 1980.

McConnell, Michael. "Religious Freedom at a Crossroads." *University of Chicago Law Review* 59 (1992): 115–94.

McKenzie, Steven L. "Deuteronomistic History." In *The Anchor Bible Dictionary*, volume 2, edited by David Noel Freedman et al., 160–68. New York: Doubleday, 1992.

McKenzie, Steven L. "Review of 'The Bible and Its Influence.'" *SBL Forum*. http://www.sbl-site.org/publications/article.aspx?articleId=465.

Moore, Diane L. *Overcoming Religious Illiteracy: A Cultural Studies Approach to the Study of Religion in Secondary Education*. New York: Palgrave, 2007.

Nash, Robert J., and Penny A. Bishop. *Teaching Adolescents Religious Literacy in a Post-9/11 World*. Charlotte, NC: IAP, 2009.

National Center for Education Statistics, Institute of Education Statistics. *Issue Brief*. December 2008. NCES 2009-039.

National Center for Education Statistics. *Homeschooling in the United States: 2003. Statistical Analysis Report*. U.S. Department of Education. Institute of Education Statistics. NCES 2006–42.

National Center for Education Statistics. *The Condition of Education 2009: Indicator 6. Homeschooled Students*. U.S. Department of Education. Institute of Education Statistics. 2009–81.

National Council on Bible Curriculum in Public Schools. *The Bible in History & Literature*. Greensboro, NC: National Council on Bible Curriculum in Public Schools, 2003–5.

National Council for the Social Studies. "Study about Religions in the Social Studies Curriculum." 1998. http://www.socialstudies.org/positions/religion.

National Education Association, Educational Policies Commission. *Moral and Spiritual Values in the Public Schools*. Washington, D.C.: National Education Association, 1951.

Neff, James Alan, Clayton T. Schorkey, and Liliane Cambraia Windsor. "Contrasting Faith-Based and Traditional Substance Abuse Treatment Programs." *Journal of Substance Abuse Treatment* 30 (2006): 49–61.

Nicholson, Ernest. *The Pentateuch in the Twentieth Century: The Legacy of Julius Wellhausen*. Oxford: Clarendon Press, 1998.

Noddings, Nel. *Educating for Intelligent Belief or Unbelief*. New York: Teachers College Press, 1993.

Nord, Warren. *Religion and American Education: Rethinking a National Dilemma*. Chapel Hill: University of North Carolina Press, 1995.

Nord, Warren. "Religion, Pluralism, and Public Education in America." *Religion and Education* 32 (2005): 11–22.

Nord, Warren A. *Does God Make a Difference? Taking Religion Seriously in Our Schools and Universities*. New York: Oxford University Press, 2010.

Nord Warren A., and Charles C. Haynes. *Taking Religion Seriously Across the Curriculum*. Nashville: Association for Curriculum Development and the First Amendment Center, 1998.

Norris, Chuck. "Bringing the Bible Back into Public Schools." *World Net Daily*, April 9, 2007. http://www.wnd.com/news/article.asp?ARTICLE_ID=55090.

Norris, Chuck. "Don't Mess with Texas . . . Textbooks!" *World Net Daily*, March 15, 2010. http://www.wnd.com/index.php?fa=PAGE.view&pageId=127935.

The One-Year Chronological Bible. The Entire New International Version in 365 Daily Readings. Carol Stream, IL: Tyndale, 1984.

Peckham, Brian. *The Composition of the Deuteronomistic History.* Harvard Semitic Monographs, 35. Atlanta: Scholars Press, 1985.

People for the American Way. *Religion in North Carolina's Schools: The Hidden Reality. A Report by the North Carolina Project of People for the American Way, September, 1983.* Winston-Salem, NC, 1983.

Prothero, Stephen. *Religious Literacy: What Every American Needs to Know—and Doesn't.* New York: Harper, 2007.

Rad, Gerhard von. "The Deuteronomic Theology of History in I and II Kings." In idem, *The Problem of the Hexateuch and Other Essays,* translated by E. Dicken, 205–21. Edinburgh/New York: Phoenician, 1966.

Rad, Gerhard von. *Old Testament Theology.* 2 vols. Translated by D.M.G. Stalker. New York: Harper & Row, 1962.

Rodgers, Ann. "Textbook Aims to Teach Bible with No Religion." *Pittsburgh Post-Gazette,* October 24, 2005. http://www.post-gazette.com/pg/05297/593949.stm.

Roncace, Mark, and Patrick Gray, eds. *Teaching the Bible: Practical Strategies for Classroom Instruction.* Atlanta: Society of Biblical Literature, 2005.

Rosenblith, Suzanne, and Scott Priestman. "Problematizing Religious Truth: Implications for Public Education." *Educational Theory* 54 (2004): 365–80.

Schafer, Marjorie Haney. *The Bible and Its Influence.* Teacher's Edition. New York and Front Royal, VA: BLP Publishing, 2006.

Schippe Cullen, and Chuck Stetson, eds. *The Bible and Its Influence.* New York and Front Royal, VA: BLP Publishing, 2006.

Siegel, Jennifer. "Bible Guide for Public Schools Gets Jewish Okay." *Forward: The Jewish Daily,* December 30, 2005. http://www.forward.com/articles/1830/.

Taylor, Charles. *Multiculturalism and the Politics of Recognition.* Princeton, NJ: Princeton University Press, 1992.

Van Biema, David. "The Case for Teaching the Bible." *Time,* April 2, 2007, 40–46. http://www.time.com/time/magazine/article/0,9171,1601845–2,00.html.

Van Biema, David. "Alabama Picks a Bible Textbook." *Time,* October 22, 2007. http://www.time.com/time/nation/article/0,8599,1674427,00.html.

Vickery, William, and Stewart G. Cole. *Intercultural Education in American Schools: Proposed Objectives and Methods.* New York and London: Harper and Brothers, 1943.

Webb, Stephen H. "The Supreme Court and the Pedagogy of Religious Studies: Constitutional Parameters for the Teaching of Religion in Public Schools." *Journal of the American Academy of Religion* 70 (2002): 135–57.

Weigle, Luther A. "Public Education and Religion." *Religious Education* 35 (1940): 67–75.

Wexler, J. D. "Preparing for the Clothed Public Square: Teaching about Religion, Civic Education, and the Constitution." *William and Mary Law Review* 43 (2002): 1161–1263.

Wind, Andrew. "Waterloo Will Not Consider High School Bible Class." WCFCourier.com, October 12, 2008.

Wuthnow, Robert. *The Restructuring of American Religion: Society and Faith since World War II*. Princeton, NJ: Princeton University Press, 1988.

Wuthnow, Robert. *America and the Challenges of Religious Diversity*. Princeton, NJ: Princeton University Press, 2005.

INDEX